Arizona Real Estate
Exam Study Guide

Jonathan Dalton

Associate Broker, REALTOR

Arizona Real Estate Exam Study Guide

ISBN 978-0-578-56229-2

Copyright © 2019, J.P. Dalton

Contents

Introduction

Before we get into the material, **congratulations!** Simply surviving the 90 hours of education required to get your real estate licenses is an accomplishment onto itself, regardless of whether you selected the classroom or online option.

Needless to say, there is a small ton of material that comes at you during the 90 hours. Hopefully your instructors, as they taught the material to you, used real life examples and other metaphors to help you understand those topics.

With that behind you, all that separates you from your real estate license is the state licensing exam and/or the school exam, depending on where you are in the process.

That's where this book comes in.

I am not going to attempt to reteach you all the material you've already seen and heard in class. You have a textbook or other material, along with your notes, that will do that for you. What I am going to do is take that 90 hours of material and condense it down to a much more manageable level of testable concepts.

Chapters are broken down according to the Arizona Department of Real Estate's licensing curriculum, so concepts may be presented in a different order than what you have seen before.

When possible, I will reduce the concepts down to bullet points that you will need to know. Examples will be given as we go, similar to the examples I used successfully in my own real estate licensing classes.

I intentionally did not include sample tests for one important reason. When I teach licensing classes, I emphasize learning the concept, not studying to answer a specific question. **If you understand the overall concept, it won't matter what question you see regarding that concept – you're prepared.** If you're trying to memorize possible questions, you are focusing on the wrong thing.

With that, if you are ready, turn the page and let's get to work helping you pass the Arizona real estate licensing exam!

Oh, and one request. When you pass the test, please drop a review on Amazon to share the great news.

Basic Testing Concepts

The best part about the Arizona real estate licensing exam is that it is a multiple-choice test. So, no matter what, the right answer is going to waiting for you among the choices. Which brings me to the most important concepts in this book:

READ THE FULL QUESTION
READ ALL THE ANSWERS

This cuts to the idea of why I didn't include practice tests. Those tests are extremely valuable in helping you get an idea of where you are and what you know. But after a while, you're going to end up memorizing those questions. And when you've done that, when you know the answer to that question three words in, you're done for. At least, unless the exam question happens to be the same question you memorized.

READ THE FULL QUESTION
READ ALL THE ANSWERS

Test writers like to put a probable but incorrect answer under choice A, knowing there will be some, through nerves or cockiness, who will jump immediately to that answer without having read the full question or the other choices.

This usually is where my students scream "trick question!" **THERE ARE NO TRICK QUESTIONS.** The questions may be nuanced, asking about one or two specific concepts that require a specific answer, but they aren't designed to fool you. In fact, sometimes the right answer will repeat key words from the question.

Two other things to keep in mind …

WATCH OUT FOR THE WORDS "NOT" AND "EXCEPT." These will trip you up if you're not careful and not reading the question fully. Don't let your chance to pass slip away because you missed a "not" or an "except" in the question.

Lastly, there is a pattern to multiple-choice tests. Two of the four choices usually are terrible. Eliminate those two first, and you're down to a coin flip. When you're only choosing among two choices, odds are you'll select the one. Just don't keep guessing C when you're stuck. That's a myth. Sorta. B also works in those situations.

Chapter 1
Real Estate Statutes

By far, the most heavily tested concepts on the Arizona real estate salesperson licensing exam deal with the laws of the real estate business. Which makes perfect sense, if you think about it. Before you begin selling real estate in Arizona, you need to understand the basic structure of the real estate business in this state.

Sources of Arizona Real Estate Law

Arizona Constitution Article XXVI

Here is what Article XXVI says:

> 1. Powers of real estate broker or salesman
>
> Section 1. Any person holding a valid license as a real estate broker or a real estate salesman regularly issued by the Arizona State Real Estate Department when acting in such capacity as broker or salesman for the parties, or agent for one of the parties to a sale, exchange, or trade, or the renting and leasing of property, shall have the right to draft or fill out and complete, without charge, any and all instruments incident thereto including, but not limited to, preliminary purchase agreements and earnest money receipts, deeds, mortgages, leases, assignments, releases, contracts for sale of realty, and bills of sale.

KEY IDEA TO REMEMBER:
- Article XXVI of the Arizona Constitution allows licensed salespeople to write real estate contracts from scratch as long as:
  - o The salesperson's broker is representing one of the parties in the transaction
  - o The salesperson does not charge for document preparation
  - o The salesperson does not provide legal advice

Article XXVI is what makes selling real estate in Arizona unique. In most states, licensees only can fill out preprinted forms created through statute or the local association or create letters of intent that are handed over to attorneys to turn into contracts. While free-handing a contract is highly discouraged because of liability issues, in Arizona, it's legal for a licensed salesperson to do so.

Other sources of Arizona real estate law

Arizona real estate licensees also need to follow applicable federal laws, such as the **Fair Housing Act** and **Sherman Antitrust Act**, as well as state statute and local ordinances. In addition, the real estate business can be shaped by **case law – legal precedents set through court decisions**.

Arizona Department of Real Estate

The Arizona Department of Real Estate is the administrative department charged with regulating the real estate business in the state.

KEY IDEA TO REMEMBER:
- The purpose of the Arizona Department of Real Estate is to protect the public.

Arizona Real Estate Commissioner

The Arizona Department of Real Estate is led by the Arizona real estate commissioner.

KEY IDEA TO REMEMBER:
- The commissioner is appointed by the governor and serves at the pleasure of the governor.
- The commissioner does not have a set term of office.

The commissioner cannot write real estate statutes – that is the purview of the Arizona Legislature – but the commissioner and the department are responsible for enforcing those statutes.

Also, the commissioner can develop non-statutory rules and regulations – commissioner's rules, for short, that carry the full force and effect of law.

KEY IDEAS TO REMEMBER:
- Commissioner's rules have the full force and effect of law.
- The legislature develops statutes, the commissioner and department develop commissioner's rules.

The department also can develop **Substantive Policy Statements**, which serve as best practices for the Arizona real estate industry. While there's no legal impact for not following the Substantive Policy Statements, as a matter of common sense, if the regulatory agency for the real estate business says you should do something a certain way, do it that way.

The commissioner has broad authority to regulate the real estate industry in Arizona.

The commissioner regulates not only real estate licensees, but also membership camping and cemetery sales brokers salespersons, developers and subdividers.

KEY IDEAS TO REMEMBER:
- The commissioner CAN investigate any licensee at any time for any reason.
- The commissioner MUST investigate upon receipt of a written complaint.
- In the case of a written compliant, the licensee has 14 days to respond to the department.
- In the event of an administrative hearing, the licensee has the right to an attorney.
- The commissioner can temporarily suspend a salesperson's license OR permanently revoke a license, but only after a hearing.
- The commissioner also can levy a maximum administrative penalty of $1,000 per violation.
- If an alleged infraction is of a serious nature, the commissioner can refer the investigation to the Arizona Attorney General.
- If the Attorney General brings a case, it will be presented in front of an administrative law judge. However, the final decision on discipline remains with the Commissioner, who will issue a Commissioner's Final Order.

The commissioner also can **negotiate a consent order**, issue a **non-disciplinary letter of concern** or issue a **provisional license**, all after a hearing.

Arizona Real Estate Advisory Board
KEY IDEAS TO REMEMBER:
- The Arizona real estate advisory board consists of 10 members, all appointed by the governor. One of the members must be a multi-family broker.
- The purpose of the advisory board is to advise and evaluate the commissioner.

Licensing
There are three levels of real estate licensing in the state of Arizona.

An entity license is acquired by an employing broker. This is the brokerage for whom you work. There are no education or testing requirements to obtain an entity license.

A broker's license entitles the holder to serve as a designated, managing or associate broker as well as sell real estate in Arizona.

KEY IDEAS TO REMEMBER:

- To obtain a broker's license, the applicant must have been active full-time in the real estate business for three of the past five years, verified by the applicant's broker.
- The applicant must complete 90 hours of licensing courses, either in person or online.
- A broker's license is valid for two years and expires on the last day of the month in which it was obtained.
- To maintain the license, the broker must complete 30 hours of continuing education every two years. (If the broker has no designated broker responsibilities, 24 hours of CE is required.

A sales associate's license entitles the holder to sell real estate in Arizona.

KEY IDEAS TO REMEMBER:
- To obtain a sales associate's license, the applicant must be at least 18 years of age and complete 90 hours of prelicensing courses, either in person or online.
- A sales associate's license is valid for two years and expires on the last day of the month in which it was obtained.
- To maintain the license, the sales associate must complete 24 hours of continuing education every two years.

The applicant's state exam scores or valid for one year. A sales associate can file their application and "activate" their license at the Department of Real Estate, though they will remain in inactive status until hired by an employing broker. Inactive licenses can remain so indefinitely.

A real estate license is not required for an attorney reviewing paperwork in their capacity as an attorney, by an individual buying or selling properties for themselves among other exemptions.

A real estate license is required by anyone discussing price, terms, conditions or availability of real property. Unlicensed assistants can perform the following activities, among others:

- Clerical/administrative tasks including filing, copying, mailing, scanning, answering phones, forwarding calls or transcribing callers' information for licensee
- Preparing marketing materials approved by the Designated Broker
- Set or confirm appointments for:
  - A licensee to list or show property

- A buyer with a loan officer
- A property inspector to inspect a home
- A repair/maintenance person to perform repairs/maintenance
- An appraiser to appraise property

KEY IDEAS TO REMEMBER:
- Only persons with an active real estate license can receive compensation.
- Sales associates only can practice real estate under supervision of a designated broker.
- For real estate teams, ALL team members must work for the same employing brokerage.
- Practicing real estate in Arizona without a license is a Class 6 felony.
- Auctioneers selling real property need an active real estate license.
- Sales associates only can form a Professional Limited Liability Company (PLLC), not an LLC because they are working under an existing company structure.

A licensed real estate sales associate only can work for one employing broker at a time **UNLESS** the sales associate also is performing membership camping and/or cemetery sales. In those instances, the sales associate can have separate employing brokers for each function.

A real estate designated broker can supervise real estate sales associates and brokers, membership camping sales and brokers and cemetery sales associates and brokers.

There are many, many reasons the commissioner can suspend, revoke or decline to issue a license. Here are just a few, per ARS 32-2153:

o Pursued a course of misrepresentation or made false promises, either directly or through others, whether acting in the role of a licensee or a principal in a transaction.

o Acted for more than one party in a transaction without the knowledge or consent of all parties to the transaction.

o Accepted compensation as a licensee for the performance of any of the acts specified in this chapter from any person other than the licensed broker to whom the licensee is licensed

o Represented or attempted to represent a broker other than the broker to whom the salesperson or associate broker is licensed.

o Paid or received any rebate, profit, compensation or commission in violation of statute.

- o Placed a sign on any property offering it for sale or for rent without the written authority of the owner or the owner's authorized agent.
- o Failed to keep an escrow or trust account or other record of funds deposited with the licensee relating to a real estate transaction.
- o Failed to maintain a complete record of each transaction.
- o Violated the federal fair housing law, the Arizona civil rights law or any local ordinance of a similar nature.
- o Demonstrated negligence in performing any act for which a license is required.
- o Been convicted in a court of competent jurisdiction in this or any other state of a felony or of any crime of forgery, theft, extortion, conspiracy to defraud, a crime of moral turpitude or any other like offense.
- o Made any substantial misrepresentation or made any false promises of a character likely to influence, persuade or induce.
- o Been guilty of any conduct, whether of the same or a different character than specified in this section, which constitutes fraud or dishonest dealings.

Employing/Designated broker responsibilities

Each employing broker must have a designated broker. This designated broker holds an active Arizona brokers license and is responsible for the **reasonable supervision and control of all employees of the employing broker, whether licensed or unlicensed.** Because the designated broker is liable for all of the actions of the employing broker's employees as part of their work, the designated broker has what we call **vicarious liability**.

KEY IDEAS TO REMEMBER:
- An employing broker must have an actual, bricks-and-mortar location. An employing broker cannot use pseudo-addresses (a.k.a The UPS Store or a USPS P.O. Box).
- Each employing brokerage must display both the entity license and the designated broker's license in a prominent location.
- An employing broker may have branch offices. These branch offices must have at least one employee – either a licensed sales associate or broker, who will serve as office manager.

Broker absences

There always needs to be someone watching the business. If a designated broker is going to be unavailable for more than **24 hours**, they need to appoint someone to watch the business in their stead. The appointee can be either an associated broker or sales associate of the brokerage or a designated broker of a competing brokerage. This appointment cannot last more than **30 days**.

KEY IDEA TO REMEMBER:
- The designated broker may appoint someone to watch the business. However, the designated broker still is responsible for all that takes place, even when on vacation.
- Tasks can be delegated, not the ultimate responsibility.

Temporary Brokers License

If a designated broker dies or is declared incompetent or insane, a responsible party can apply to the Arizona Department of Real Estate for a temporary brokers license. This responsible party need not be licensed. For example, the spouse of the deceased designated broker can obtain the license. The sole purpose of the temporary brokers license is winding down and closing out the business.

KEY IDEAS TO REMEMBER:
- The temporary brokers license is valid for 90 days.
- The temporary brokers license can be extended out for a maximum of 15 months.
- The temporary broker cannot take on new business nor hire new employees.

Client Funds and Broker Trust Accounts

Real estate brokers in Arizona are NOT required to have a trust account UNLESS the brokerage will be handling client funds (i.e., property management where the broker handles rents and deposits, etc.)

Property managers MUST have a trust account.

KEY IDEAS TO REMEMBER:
- The trust account is a bank account, separate from the broker's operating accounts.
- A broker's trust account must be located within the state of Arizona, with a handful of exceptions.
- When deposits are made, the deposit slip must indicate the date, amount, account number and the principals to the transaction for which the deposit was made.

- Sales associates must deliver a buyer's earnest deposit to their broker PROMPTLY. The broker then deposits those funds in the broker's trust account or an escrow company trust account IMMEDIATELY (meaning next business day).
- Any licensed individual can be a signatory on a broker trust account. On property management trust accounts, any employee – licensed or unlicensed – can sign. Property owners never can be a signatory on a property management trust account.

Think about it. A property manager likely has more than one client. So, the individual clients cannot be signatories because they'd then have access to funds that weren't theirs.

Trust accounts may be interest bearing. The accounts must be reconciled monthly and interest has to be removed from the account at least annually.

NOTE: The broker deposit time frame for rental deposits is three business days, NOT immediately (i.e., next business day) per commissioner's rules.

There are two major do-not-do's when it comes to broker trust accounts:

- **COMMINGLING: A broker cannot have more than $3,000 of their own money in the trust account. These funds only are to be used for bank fees.**
- **CONVERSION: This is using client funds for a broker's own purposes. Depositing client funds anywhere but the trust account – in a broker's operating or personal account for example – or writing operating checks out of the trust account would be conversion violations.**

Commissions

Only actively licensed sales associates and brokers are entitled to real estate commissions. All commissions – all compensation – belongs to and is paid by the employing broker. No unlicensed or inactively licensed individuals may receive commission or other compensation.

KEY IDEAS TO REMEMBER:
- Commissions are earned when the licensee finds a ready, willing and able buyer who meets the seller's terms, NOT at close of escrow.
- Commission generally is paid at close of escrow, with exceptions for seller breach of contract.
- All compensation is paid through the employing broker for which the licensee worked when the commission was earned.

- Only actively licensed individuals can receive commission or other related compensation. NO unlicensed or inactively licensed individuals can receive commission payments.
- The licensee DOES NOT have to be actively licensed when the commission is paid, only when the commission was earned.
- THERE ARE NO STANDARD COMMISSION RATES. ALL COMMISSIONS ARE FULLY NEGOTIABLE PER THE SHERMAN ANTITRUST ACT.
- To pursue a commission in court, the licensee would need a copy of their active license and their listing agreement.
- Only the names of the brokerages receiving compensation AND representing one of the principals (buyer/seller) need be disclosed. Referral fees do not have to be disclosed to either of the principals.

Real estate licensees may not receive compensation for negotiating loans. This would require a separate mortgage loan originator or mortgage broker's license.

Actively licensed real estate professionals can refer business to out-of-state brokerages and receive a referral fee as compensation, paid through the licensee's employing broker. Out-of-state brokerages cannot practice real estate in Arizona unless licensed in Arizona.

Arizona does not require real estate licensees to live in Arizona to practice real estate here.

KEY IDEA TO REMEMBER:
- Practicing real estate license without a license is a Class 6 felony.

Subdivided Land

Arizona has a checkered past when it comes to the sale of improved and unimproved land. In a 1979 article from the Arizona Republic, it was estimated there had been approximately a half billion dollars (about $1.7 billion dollars) in fraudulent land deals during the 1960s and 1970s.

From non-existent mining claims to landlocked, worthless parcels, unscrupulous people took advantage of the public at an alarming rate. To combat this history, the state Legislature enacted extremely strict laws regarding the subdividing and development of land.

Definitions

When most of us think of the term subdivision, we think of the neighborhoods in which we live. But subdivided land had a specific meaning. **Subdividing land is defined as dividing one large parcel into six or more smaller parcels.**

With subdivision laws, this general definition is broken down even further:

KEY IDEAS TO REMEMBER:
- "Lot splits" consist of one parcel divided into 5 or fewer parcels.
- "Subdivided land" consists of 6 or more parcels, all of fewer than 36 acres.
- "Unsubdivided land" consists of 6 or more parcels, all of between 36 and 159.9 acres.
- "Bulk land" consists of one parcel or more than 160 acres.

On the vast majority of real property transactions, the buyer does not have a rescission period – an opportunity to change one's mind, simply put. But buyers do have a rescission period on certain land deals.

First, though, we need two more definitions:

KEY IDEAS TO REMEMBER:
- An "improved lot" either has a structure or an existing contract to build a structure within the next two years.
- An "unimproved lot" doesn't.

Let's now merge the above to bring in the rescission periods.

KEY IDEAS TO REMEMBER:
- Subdivided, improved lots have NO rescission period.
- Subdivided, unimproved lots have a six-month rescission period sight unseen, seven days once inspected.
- **ALL** unsubdivided lots (either improved or unimproved) have a six-month rescission period sight unseen, seven days once inspected.

One final pair of definitions – the **subdivider** is the person who divides the land. The **developer** is the person who then develops or improves the property. No real estate license is required to subdivide or develop real property in Arizona.

Public Reports

Subdividers and developers are subject to statutes requiring detailed disclosure about their project and themselves. Before a subdivider can begin selling either **subdivided** or **unsubdivided land**, they must complete, and submit to the Department of Real Estate for approval, a Public Report.

KEY IDEA TO REMEMBER:

- The public report requirement applies **ONLY** to residential properties, not commercial or industrial.

There are about two dozen items that the public report must contain, but these are the most relevant for our purposes:

- The subdivider cannot have prior fraud convictions.
- The subdivider must be able to provide the buyer with marketable title – title free and clear of any undisclosed defects or issues that could impact the buyer's ability to sell at a later date.
- The subdivider must provide permanent access – ingress and egress – to the parcel.
- The public report must include a full title report, legal descriptions, approximate real estate taxes and the status of any planned improvements.
- The public report must include information about the presence of military or other airports, earth fissures or expansive soil.

The subdivider would not include floor plans, for instance, as those are largely irrelevant from a larger disclosure perspective.

KEY IDEAS TO REMEMBER:

- Once approved by the Department, a public report is valid for five years unless there have been substantive changes made.
- If ownership changes, the Department may allow the new subdivider to utilize the previously issued public report through a Subsequent Owner Exception.

Public reports are not required on lot splits (i.e., a larger parcel divided into five or fewer parcels). In this instance, the seller would provide an **Affidavit of Disclosure**. This Affidavit of Disclosure essentially is a mini public report.

KEY IDEA TO REMEMBER:

- Affidavits of Disclosure are required on sales of five or fewer parcels in unincorporated area, not in a subdivision.

In other words, an Affidavit of Disclosure would not be used in Sun City, which is unincorporated but organized in subdivisions, but would be used in Wittman in the Northwest Valley or county islands between Mesa and Apache Junction near the Superstition Mountains.

Lot Reservations

A subdivider CANNOT sell any lots until the public report had been approved by the Department. The subdivider CAN, however, accept lot reservations.

KEY IDEA TO REMEMBER:
- A subdivider can accept a fully-refundable lot reservation deposit of not more than $5,000.
- This lot reservation deposit must be kept in a neutral escrow account.

Rescission Period – Public Report
KEY IDEAS TO REMEMBER:
- The subdivider must have the buyer sign a receipt showing that the buyer has received the public report.
- The subdivider must retain these public report receipts for five years.
- The buyer has a three-year rescission period if he/she is not provided with a public report before purchasing from a subdivider.

Final Thoughts
There are a number of ways you could be asked a question regarding subdivision definitions:

- A person can subdivide and sell up to five lots without needing a pubic report.
- Someone who owns six lots and wishes to sell just one still would need a public report.

Real Estate Recovery Fund
The Arizona Legislature created a Real Estate Recovery Fund. This fund, administered by the Department and the Commissioner, is designed to provide financial relief for those who suffered financial losses due to the actions of a real estate licensee.

KEY IDEAS TO REMEMBER:

- The fund is funded through fees charged when prospective licensees apply to the department.
- Sales associates pay $10. Brokers pay $20. This generally is a one-time fee.
- The fund must have a balance of at least $600,000 on June 30, the final day of the state's fiscal year.
- If the balance is below $600,000, all licensees pay an additional $10/$20 when they renew.
- The maximum payment per claimant per transaction is $30,000. (If there are five buyers on the same contract, they are considered one claimant.)
- The maximum payment for the life of a licensee is $90,000.
- Only natural persons can make claims on the fund – no corporations or LLCs.
- Only transactions for real property in Arizona are eligible for payment. However, the claimant does not need to live in Arizona.
- Once payment has been made from the recovery fund, the licensee's license is terminated.

Unlike a revoked license, which is permanently gone, a terminated license **can** be resurrected. The licensee would have to **pay the recovery fund back in full, plus 10 percent annual interest**, before applying. The commissioner can **deny the application** for up to **five years after payment is made.**

Chapter 2
Commissioner's Rules

While the Arizona Legislature passes statutes, the real estate commissioner can develop rules and regulations. These rules and regulations, located in Title 4, Chapter 28 of the Arizona Administrative Code, carry the full force and effect of law even though they aren't statutes.

1. Licensing

The majority of licensing rules are covered under Real Estate Statutes. However, there are a few items which appear in commissioner's rules alone.

The first is the **"10 calendar day" rule**. In virtually all situations where a brokerage or licensee needs to notify the Department of changes, the notification must take place within 10 calendar days. Among the items covered under the **10-calendar day rule**:

- If a brokerage changes location, the Department must be notified within 10 calendar days
- If a licensee leaves a brokerage, the broker has 10 calendar days to return the license
- If a licensee's business information changes … 10 calendar days to notify
- If a licensee is found guilty of, pleads no contest to or reaches a plea agreement on any felony or criminal misdemeanor … 10 calendar days to notify
- If a judgment is recorded against a licensee … 10 calendar days to notify

If a licensee elects to form a limited liability company for business purposes, it must be formed as a PLLC – a professional limited liability company.

2. Branch Offices

All branch offices need to have at least one employee; this could be the branch manager. The branch manager can be either a licensed sales associate or licensed broker, though a licensed sales associate cannot review paperwork or hire other licensees.

Branch offices must have a sign indicating that this is a branch office along with the name of the office manager. Branch offices must have a separate branch office license.

KEY IDEAS TO REMEMBER:

- Branch offices must have a separate license, signage and an office manager.
- The office manager can be a licensed sales associate or licensed broker.
- If a brokerage closes a branch office without notifying the department, the brokerage is subject to disciplinary action, including a civil penalty of up to $1,000.

3. Advertising

All advertising falls under the supervision of the designated broker as part of the broker's reasonable supervision and control. In addition to Fair Housing and other real estate statutes, licensees need to be aware of several Commissioner's Rules regarding advertising:

KEY IDEAS TO REMEMBER:
- All advertisements must include the broker's business name, placed in a clear and prominent manner. Advertisements that do not include the broker's business name are considered illegal "blind ads."
- There is no requirement regarding font size or style for the broker's business name.
- A licensee, when selling his own property, must disclose that they own the property. All advertising must include the phrase "owner/agent" and any for sale sign must include a sign rider that says "owner/agent."
- When advertising another licensee's listing, the name of the listing brokerage must be clearly displayed.
- When advertising an "acre," the parcel MUST be 43,560 square feet. Anything less than a full acre cannot be advertised as an "acre".
- Licensees must have the written consent of a property owner to advertise their property. This includes placement of a "for sale" sign on the property.

When giving away a promotional item such as a gift card, the licensee **must disclose the value** of the item, **how many are available** and **what must be done** to obtain the item. The name of the store of the restaurant **does not need to be disclosed.** Finally, while time share developers and subdividers can hold lottery drawings with Department approval, individual licensees may not.

4. Handling Offers

Offers are best viewed in terms of real estate sales rather than leases as that is what the vast majority of real estate licensees will see most often.

An **offer** is exactly that – an offer made by a buyer to purchase real property. The seller can either accept, reject or amend that offer. If amended, the buyer's original offer is terminated and in its place is the **counteroffer**.

Our "ORs" and "Ees" apply when discussing the parties involved with an offer. The party making the offer is the **offeror**. The party receiving the offer is the **offeree.** While the buyer begins as the offeror and the seller as the offeree, these roles can change with every counter offer in a negotiation.

 KEY IDEAS TO REMEMBER:
- The listing broker is responsible for presenting all offers.
- In Arizona, all offers must be presented through the close of escrow UNLESS the seller has given their broker written permission to withhold once an offer has been accepted.
- In Arizona, verbal offers must be presented through the close of escrow UNLESS the seller has given their broker written permission with withhold verbal offers.
- The client (buyer/seller) decides whether to accept an offer or counteroffer. Brokers will assist in negotiation, but cannot accept or reject an offer on their clients' behalf.
- Brokers must ensure the participating parties receive copies of all executed paperwork.

All negotiations are to be conducted through the client's broker. The only time a buyer's agent can present an offer directly to a seller whose home is listed through a brokerage is if that broker or any licensee of the brokerage cannot be contacted within 24 hours. In that case, the buyer's agent can present an offer directly to the seller **with the written permission of the seller.**

Additional Concepts About Offers
KEY IDEAS TO REMEMBER:
- The listing broker must present all offers as soon as possible.
- If the listing broker has received multiple offers, these need to be presented to the seller as simultaneously as possible.
- The offeror can withdraw their offer at any time before it is has been accepted
  - o If the offeror puts a three-day response deadline on their offer, they don't have to wait the full three days before withdrawing their offer.

- Offers only are valid until the deadline on the offer – this is one meaning of "time is of the essence."
- Buyers must disclose in writing when they are making offers on multiple properties at the same time.

The Arizona Association of REALTORS has created a Multiple Counteroffer form. Using this form, a seller can counter multiple offers simultaneously. The terms offered in each counter do not need the same; the seller can write a separate counter to each buyer. The form, however, discloses the fact that the seller is countering multiple offers and no offer will be deemed accepted until the seller has signed a second time after buyer acceptance.

5. Professional Conduct

Arizona Commissioner's rule R-4-28-1101 contains nearly a dozen different provisions regarding professional conduct. Rather than quote the rule in full, here are the basics you will need to know:

KEY IDEAS TO REMEMBER:
- Licensees owe a fiduciary duty to their client (we will discuss more in Chapter 4, Agency Law).
- Licensees must disclose all known material facts and defects about the property in writing.
  - o A material fact is any information that would impact a buyer's decision to purchase or what price they might pay for the property.
  - o Licensees are held to the legal standard of what they knew or should have known.
- Licensees must "expeditiously perform" all of their duties.
- Licensees never can allow a commission dispute to delay or interfere with a transaction.
- Licensees must disclose whether they have a financial interest in any property being sold or purchased.
  - o Licensees cannot buy properties they are negotiating to list for the seller unless they disclose their potential interest to purchase up front.
  - o Licensees, when selling their own property, must advertise as "Owner/Agent," including an "Owner/Agent" sign rider if a sign is installed.

- Licensees must disclose whether they are related to one of the parties in the transaction. (i.e., buyer/seller is related to licensed real estate agent/broker in the state of Arizona.)
- Licensees will not provide advice or otherwise provide services outside their areas of expertise. ALWAYS advise your clients to pursue legal or other advice as they feel necessary.
- Licensees can neither advertise for sale nor place a for sale sign on any real property without written authorization of the owner.

Broker Supervision and Control

KEY IDEAS TO REMEMBER:

- A designated broker must review and initial/sign all paperwork within 10 business days.
- Brokers must keep copies of executed contracts for five years from termination.
- Brokers must keep copies of rejected offers for one year.
  - o The paperwork does not need to be kept on site, but must be accessible by the department in case of audit.
- Brokers must have an Office Policies and Procedures manual, which outlines the rules of the road for the brokerage and its associated licensees and unlicensed employees.
  - o Self-employed brokers with no more than one licensee and one unlicensed employee are exempt from the policies and procedure manual requirement.
- Brokers must either maintain a physical copy of the Arizona Real Estate Law book or provide internet access so licensees/employees can access the electronic copy on the Department site.
- If a designated broker will be out of pocket for 24 hours or more, they must appoint someone to supervise the business. The designated broker remains liable for any actions of any licensed or unlicensed employees.
  - o The above appointment cannot last for more than 30 days.

Chapter 3
Agency Law

Agency can be one of the most complicated concepts in real estate because people are complicated. Fortunately, the real estate exam doesn't delve into the complications. In fact, the basic structure of agency is remarkably simple.

When one person hires another into a relationship of trust and confidence, this is agency. We refer to that **relationship of trust and confidence** as a **fiduciary relationship.**

The person who hires another to represent them is the **principal** or **client**.

The person who is hired is the **agent**. Since, in Arizona, all transactions are handled at the broker level, the agent for the client is the **designated broker** NOT the sales associate. The agent, in representing the client, must put the client's best interest first, even ahead of the agent's best interest.

Any third party to the transaction not represented by the agent is considered a **customer**.

Simply put … **We work FOR our client and we work a customer.**

KEY IDEA TO REMEMBER:
- Designated brokers have vicarious liability for the actions of the brokerage's employees during the course of their business. In other words, the designated broker is responsible for all actions taken in the course of business even though the designated broker likely was unaware of what was taking place.

Fiduciary Duties

Licensees are supposed to discuss representation and agency the first time that they meet with a prospective client.

When hired by a principal, the agent owes the client a wide variety of fiduciary duties. The best way to remember these duties is the mnemonic **CARLOAD**. Each letter is the first letter of one of the seven fiduciary responsibilities:

Confidentiality

Accounting

Reasonable care

Loyalty

Obedience

Advocacy

Disclosure

KEY IDEAS TO REMEMBER:
- All of the above fiduciary duties end when the agency relationship ends EXCEPT confidentiality. Confidentiality lasts forever.
- Obedience applies only to lawful and ethical instructions of the client. Licensees are not required to follow any unlawful or unethical instructions
  - o A seller cannot demand an agent not show their home to members of a protected class, as this violates Fair Housing.
  - o A seller cannot order their agent not to disclose a material fact or defect, such as a crack in the foundation, as this violates the agent's legal disclosure obligations.

Confidentiality includes protecting your client's personal identifying information to help prevent **identity theft**. Securely dispose of all paperwork and electronic files that contain your client's personal identifying information and make sure all such paperwork is secured at day's end (i.e., placed in a locked drawer or cabinet.)

Licensees also should make sure their clients do not obey any wire instructions they receive verbally or via e-mail without verifying the information with their bank and the escrow company. This will help prevent **wire fraud**.

2. Agency Basics

Below is a basic sketch of the agency structure from the perspective of a seller listing their home:

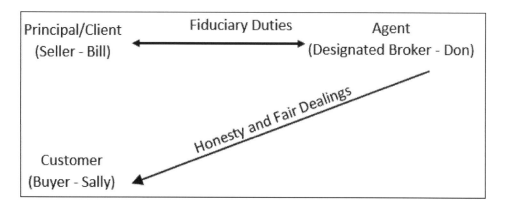

Bill, our seller, is hiring ABC Realty to list his home. Don is the designated broker for ABC Realty – Don's employing broker – so Bill is hiring Don to be his "agent." Don has a fiduciary responsibility to Bill and must put Bill's best interest ahead of anyone else's, including Don's.

Sally, the buyer, is a third party to the transaction not represented by Don and ABC Realty and is a customer. As such, Don owes her honesty and fair dealings but not the full fiduciary responsibilities.

3. Types of Agency

Special Agency

Special agency takes place when the agent (in Arizona, the designated broker), is representing the client in **one and only one real property transaction**. Special agency transactions are one-and-done deals; the agent helps the client purchase or sell one and only one specific property. **Special agency is not ongoing**.

General Agency

In a **general agency** relationship, the agent (in Arizona, the designated broker), is representing the client in a wide variety of real estate transactions. The key concept with general agency is that it is an ongoing relationship.

There are two main scenarios where we see general agency applied in real estate.

The first is **property management.** Property managers represent their property owners on an ongoing basis. They do not need to seek permission to fill vacancies, have repairs made, etc. The authority is ongoing.

The second is a **sales associate's relationship to their designated broker**. The licensee does not need the permission of the designated broker every time they list a home for sale or meet with a potential buyer. The licensee's authority to represent their designated broker in client acquisition is ongoing.

Universal Agency

In a **universal agency** relationship, the fiduciary or agent represents the client in all aspects of their life. The agent has **unlimited authority** to act on the client's behalf. To become a universal agent, the client must sign a **power of attorney** form, which makes the agent an **attorney-in-fact**.

KEY IDEA TO REMEMBER:
- The Power of attorney is a form. The person named by the client becomes an attorney-in-fact.

Single agency

Single agency is the most common type of agency representation. In single agency, the agent (in Arizona, the designated broker), **represents only one party in the transaction** – either the buyer or the seller, or either the landlord or the tenant.

Dual agency

Dual agency, commonly referred to limited representation in Arizona, takes place when the agent (in Arizona, the designated broker), **represents both parties to a transaction** – buyer AND seller, or landlord AND tenant. Because all clients are represented at the brokerage level, dual agency can take place with both one licensee, or two licensees working under the same designated broker.

KEY IDEA TO REMEMBER:
- To perform dual agency, the agent must obtain PRIOR, WRITTEN, INFORMED consent of both parties to the transaction.

4. Additional Agency Concepts

Due Diligence

Real estate licensees in Arizona need to provide the reasonable care – a basic level of skill, knowledge and competence – that any client should rightfully expect. However, this obligation on the part of the licensee does not relieve the client's responsibility to perform their own **due diligence**.

✳ KEY IDEA TO REMEMBER:

- Due diligence is the basic inspection, review and homework any reasonable person would undertake before purchasing a parcel of real property.

Puffing

Puffing is legally exaggerated opinion. The idea is if an agent says "you can eat off these floors" to emphasize how clean they are, the buyer can't sue the agent if they try to eat off the floors and get sick.

Misrepresentation and Fraud

Misrepresentation is an innocent misstatement of fact. For example, a buyer asks their agent if all the appliances are gas. The agent looks at the MLS sheet, sees gas heat, a gas water heater and a gas stove, and answers yes. The client later discovers the dryer runs on electric, not gas. The agent's error could be regarded as misrepresentation, as it was an unintentional error.

Fraud, sometimes known as **negligent misrepresentation**, is a deliberate misstatement with the intent to deceive for personal or financial gain. **Culpable negligence** – acting with a blatant disregard for the truth – also would fall under the category of fraud.

✳ KEY IDEA TO REMEMBER:

- The difference between misrepresentation and fraud is intent.

Brokers usually will carry **errors and omissions insurance** – similar to the malpractice insurance that doctors carry. E&O insurance **will** cover misrepresentation but **will not** cover fraud, culpable negligence or illegal activities such as violating either Fair Housing laws or the Sherman Antitrust Act.

5. Creating Agency Relationships

Agency can be created through either an **expressed** or **implied** agreement.

Expressed agency means the terms of the agency relationship have been agreed upon either verbally or in writing. Examples of written expressed agency agreements are **listing agreements** and **buyer broker agreements**. Both the listing agreement and buyer broker agreement also serve as employment contracts and are examples of personal services contracts.

All expressed employment agreements must be written in **clear and unambiguous language**, contain set **beginning and ending dates**, set forth **all terms including compensation** and **be signed by all parties**.

Implied agency means that, through their words and actions, the client and agent have created a less-than-formal agency agreement.

For example, consider a potential buyer who calls you to look at a few homes. You will show them the homes. You'll likely make comments about the homes, material facts about the area and the plusses and minuses of the property. You may even run comps on the home. You and the client have entered into an implied agency because both you and the client are acting as if you have been hired as their agent.

Terminating Agency Relationships

There are a number of ways in which agency relationships can be terminated. The most common is **performance** – either the agent has helped their buyer purchase or their seller sell a home.

KEY IDEAS TO REMEMBER:
- Agency agreements must have set timeframes, which means they can expire.
- When a client fires their agent, this is called revocation.
- When the agent fires their client, this is called renunciation.

Since agency agreements are personal services contracts, **death of the client** will terminate agency. Likewise, **death of the broker** will terminate agency, since all agreements are through the broker. Also, death of a sales associate **will not alter** the agency agreement.

Buyer Broker Agreements

A **buyer broker agreement** is an employment agreement between a buyer and a designated broker where the buyer hires the broker to help them find a home. In the buyer broker agreement, the broker can set their own commission to be paid by the buyer regardless of what is offered in the MLS, with any cooperating commission from the MLS offsetting what the buyer owes.

KEY IDEAS TO REMEMBER:
- Buyer broker agreements must have set beginning and ending dates.
- Buyer broker agreements must be signed by all parties.
- Buyer broker agreements cannot be assigned to a different designated broker.
- A licensee should not attempt to sign a client already bound under a buyer broker agreement with another brokerage, nor encourage the client to cancel their existing agreement.

Chapter 4
Listings

Listings are the life blood of the real estate industry. There's an old saying – "listers last." There are a handful of different types of listings you need to know.

Common Listing Types

Open listing – the sellers hire a number of different brokerages to sell their home. Only the brokerage that brings the buyer, that can show what we call **procuring cause**, is paid a commission.

Exclusive agency – the sellers hire one brokerage exclusively to sell their home. This broker **always** will get paid a commission **unless** the seller sells their home themselves.

KEY IDEA TO REMEMBER:
- The only time the listing broker DOES NOT get paid a commission on an exclusive agency listing is if the seller sells themselves. The broker WILL get paid if anyone other than the seller brings the buyer.

Exclusive right to sell – the sellers hire one brokerage exclusively to sell their home. This broker **always** will receive a commission. Period. End of story. Full stop.

KEY IDEA TO REMEMBER:
- The ONLY difference between exclusive agency and exclusive right to sell is that, on exclusive agency, the sellers can sell their home themselves and not pay a commission.

Net listing – the sellers hire one brokerage exclusively to sell their home. The sellers decide what they want to net from the sale and the broker's commission is whatever they get above that amount.

Net listings are illegal in many states because of the obvious possibilities for conflicts of interest. In Arizona, net listings are legal but highly discouraged by most brokerages.

KEY IDEAS TO REMEMBER:
- Open listings are unilateral contracts – only the seller is obligated to take action (i.e., pay the broker who brings the buyer).

- Exclusive agency, exclusive right to sell and net listings are bilateral contracts – both the brokerage and the seller have performance obligations.

Multiple Listing Service (MLS)

The **multiple listing service** is a place where cooperating brokerages come together, advertise their listings to each other and offer cooperative compensations to brokerages representing buyers who purchase a listing.

KEY IDEA TO REMEMBER:
- Homes cannot be entered into the MLS without an offer of cooperative compensation.

There are different ways a seller can have their home advertised in the MLS:

Full service brokerages not only advertise the home in the MLS, but also handle all other aspects of marketing and negotiation. These brokerages work hand-in-hand with the client every step of the way from listing to close of escrow.

Limited service brokerages vary widely in the services offered. MLS advertisement generally is a given, but the level of other advertising, marketing and contract negotiation varies greatly from one limited service brokerage to the next.

Additional Listing Types

There are three other types of listings, less common than the others, that you also need to know.

Pocket listings – these are listings where the broker is not advertising the home through the MLS. This usually is done for privacy reasons – your average multi-millionaire doesn't necessarily want their home details marketed to the world at large. Though not in the MLS, the listing broker generally would work with other brokerages representing buyers and offer cooperative compensation.

Exclusive listings – these are similar to pocket listings in that the broker is not advertising the home through the MLS. However, with an exclusive listing, the listing broker does not want to work with nor is offering cooperative compensation to other brokers. They are going 100 percent solo and will not work with a brokerage representing a buyer.

Coming soon listings – these are listings that aren't yet on the market. The listing agent may advertise a listing as "coming soon" via a sign rider or "delayed" in the local MLS in hopes of generating interest in the property ahead of its availability.

KEY IDEA TO REMEMBER:
- Coming soon listings can cause Fair Housing issues should the seller elect to review and/or accept offers before the home is officially "on the market." Questions could be raised about why the seller decided to look at or accept one offer but not others before the home was officially available.

Working with For Sale by Owners

Some owners elect to sell their homes themselves – the so-called FSBOs (For Sale by Owner). While these owners are not interested in being represented by a broker on the sale, many will cooperate and offer compensation with brokerages representing a buyer. Buyers agents should have these sellers sign an **Unrepresented Compensation Agreement**, which both sets the terms of compensation and makes clear that the buyer's brokerage is not representing the seller and owes no fiduciary duties to the seller.

An unrepresented seller is a **customer** only, never a **client**.

Chapter 5
Contract Law

Because real estate licensees can write contracts from scratch, with some stipulations, per Article XXVI of the Arizona Constitution, it is even more essential for potential licensees here to understand the basics of contract law.

Though licensees in Arizona can write contracts from scratch, most brokers prefer their licensees to use standard forms. These forms, particularly for residential transactions, are designed by the Arizona Association of REALTORS.

KEY IDEAS TO REMEMBER:
- The pre-printed language on the contracts is called boilerplate.
- In legal proceedings, handwritten changes to the contract have the highest precedence, followed by typed changes and then the boilerplate.
- All such changes need to be signed/initialed by both parties.
- No verbal changes can override what is in writing – this is the parol evidence rule.

Classification of Contracts

A **contract** is a legally binding agreement where two or more parties agree to do or not do something. There are several ways contracts can be classified. These are not mutually exclusive categories.

Expressed or Implied

An **expressed contract** can be either **verbal** or **written**. In either case, the full terms and conditions of the contract have to be detailed in clear and understandable language.

An **implied contract** is one where the terms simply are understood by all parties. For example, if you go to a restaurant, it's understood that you will order food, that the restaurant will make the food and, at the end of your meal, you will pay for the food. No discussion or written agreement is needed.

Unilateral or Bilateral

With a **unilateral contract**, only one party is obligated to act. For example, if my dog runs away and I offer a $50 reward to bring him home, you're not obligated to look for him. But I am obligated to pay you the promised $50 if you do bring him home.

With a **bilateral contract**, both parties have obligations. A purchase contract is a real estate bilateral contract, because ultimately the buyer and seller both have to take necessary steps to effect the sale.

Executory or Executed

An **executory contract** is one where one or more parties still have to take action for the contract to be completed. Buyer contingencies, for instance, make a real estate purchase contract executory during the escrow period.

An **executed contract** is one that has been terminated, either happily with the close of escrow or unhappily with a cancellation or breach of contract. "Executed contract" is one of the two most misused phrases in real estate; while everyone asks the licensee for a copy of the executed contract, it's not truly executed until terminated.

KEY IDEA TO REMEMBER:
- A real estate purchase contract typically is an expressed, bilateral, executory contract when first executed and becomes executed upon close of escrow, cancellation or breach.

Contract Status

Contracts can have different statuses depending on circumstance. A contract can be considered **valid**, **void**, **voidable** or **unenforceable**.

A **valid** contract is exactly what it sounds like – legally valid and fully enforceable.

A **void** contract, for our purposes, is a contract with an illegal purpose. For instance, if a buyer wants to know if the HOA will allow a 10-foot storage shed to accommodate their planned meth lab, the contract would be void from the start.

A **voidable** contract can be cancelled unilaterally by one of the parties. For our purposes, the purchase contract would be voidable because the buyer has nearly a dozen different ways they can cancel the contract unilaterally before close of escrow.

Unenforceable is a catch-all category, encompassing anything (other than an illegal purpose) that would cause a court to rule that the contract cannot be enforced. For instance, if the contract is missing one of the essential elements, it could be considered unenforceable.

Essential Elements of a Contract

For a contract to be fully enforceable, there are a number of elements that must be present.

Statute of Frauds/In Writing

The **Statute of Frauds** dates back to 1677 and was designed to prevent perjury. It's harder to lie about something when the details are in writing, unless we are on Twitter! States have their own version of the statute of frauds, including Arizona.

Per the Statute of Frauds, all real estate agreements must be in writing to be enforceable with two exceptions – leases for one year or less and broker-to-broker agreements.

KEY IDEA TO REMEMBER:

- A one-year lease doesn't need to be in writing to be enforceable. A purchase contract to buy real property does need to be in writing.

Competent Parties

All parties to a contract must be legally competent so that they understand the agreement that they are entering into. First, all parties must be of legal age. In Arizona, the **age of majority** Is 18.

KEY IDEA TO REMEMBER:

- A minor **CAN** purchase real estate in Arizona but **CANNOT** be held legally liable for the terms of the contract. If a minor enters into a real estate contract, the contract is **VOIDABLE** by the minor only until their age of majority.

Legal competence – whether someone is of sound mind – is determined by the court. Parties can be declared to be temporarily mentally incompetent because of drug or alcohol use, or because they are under duress and menace.

KEY IDEA TO REMEMBER:

- Duress is an implied threat of harm. Menace is an actual threat of harm. When a party claims they signed under duress or menace, they DO have the right to continue forward with the contract. Therefore, a contract signed under **DURESS** or **MENACE** is **VOIDABLE**.

Lawful Purpose

As mentioned previously, the contract must have a **lawful purpose** else it is considered **void**.

Offer, Acceptance and Notification

Contracts are created when there has been an **offer** made by the offeror, **acceptance** by the offeree and **notification** of the acceptance back to the offeror. Without all three – **offer**, **acceptance** and **notification** there is no contract.

KEY IDEA TO REMEMBER:

- There are a number of ways the test may ask questions regarding offer, acceptance and notification. **ALWAYS** make sure all three have taken place, otherwise there is no contract.

If notification of acceptance is given to the offeror's agent, this is considered notification to the offeror as well. This is called **imputed notice**.

For the contract to be valid, **it must be signed by all parties. Electronic signatures** are valid on nearly all real estate documents not requiring a notary.

Consideration

Consideration is something of value given in exchange for something else. For example, when buying a house, the purchase price is the consideration.

KEY IDEAS TO REMEMBER:

- Consideration does not always have to be monetary. It can be valuable or good:
    - o Valuable consideration is monetary – money, goods, services.
    - o Good consideration generally is defined as "love and affection" and is used when property is gifted, usually among relatives.

Legal Description

We will discuss legal descriptions in a later chapter. For now, know that the contract needs a valid legal description describing the real property being conveyed. This can be either a **metes and bounds**, **lot and block** or **rectangular survey**.

Contract Termination

There are a number of methods through which contracts can be terminated. The most common is **performance**. Both parties completed all of their obligations and the purpose for which the contract was created has been completed. On the less happy side, contracts also can be terminated through either **cancellation** or **breach**. Also, contracts usually contain a **'time is of the essence"** clause. This clause says all deadlines, including the close of escrow, are firm. Because of this, a contract will be considered to be expired if the stated close of escrow date has passed.

KEY IDEA TO REMEMBER:
- Once created, death of the principals to a contract will not terminate the contract. If either buyer or seller dies after the contract is created, the contract remains valid and is enforceable on the estate.
  - o There are other contract contingencies that could cause the contract to terminate, but death of the principals alone isn't sufficient to invalidate the contract.

Risk of Loss

The Arizona Association of REALTORS' Residential Resale Purchase Contract contains the following paragraph regarding the risk of loss once a contract has been created:

> **Risk of Loss:** If there is any loss or damage to the Premises between the date of Contract acceptance and COE or possession, whichever is earlier, by reason of fire, vandalism, flood, earthquake, or act of God, the risk of loss shall be on Seller, provided, however, that if the cost of repairing such loss or damage would exceed ten percent (10%) of the purchase price, either Seller or Buyer may elect to cancel the Contract.

If a seller, for instance, lights a candle and burns a hole in the laminate countertops, the seller would be required to repair the damage and the buyer would be required to purchase as before. If the property were to burn down, however, the seller doesn't have the rebuild and the buyer doesn't have to buy; the contract would be cancelled.

Additional Contract Concepts

Letter of Intent

A **letter of intent** is a non-legally binding written statement setting for the terms under which a buyer would purchase a particular property. This is not a firm offer. Rather, it is a summary of the important points used as a starting point for negotiations.

Earnest Money

Earnest money is a good faith deposit, an inducement for a seller to accept a buyer's offer. Earnest money is not legally required but, for practical purposes, a contract written without any earnest money offered is dead on arrival.

Earnest money is **NOT** consideration. Consideration is the purchase price. The earnest money is good faith money. The contract must state **what form** the earnest money will take and whether it will be deposited in the **broker's trust account** or an **escrow company's trust account**.

Deposit of the earnest money gives the buyer an **equitable interest** in the property. In other words, the property no longer is the sellers to do with what they please. For instance, a seller cannot paint the entire interior of a house under contract pink because they feel like it. The buyer's **equitable interest** is based on the concept that the real property must be in the same condition at close of escrow as it was when the contract was entered into.

Contingencies

A contract can contain any number of **contingencies**. To be valid, the contingency must state what party has to do what, when it must be done and who will cover the cost of the action.

Nominees and Assignees

A **nominee** is a third party who purchases real property on someone else's behalf as if they were purchasing the property themselves. This allows the actual buyer to remain anonymous.

An **assignee** is a third party to whom the buyer assigns her interest in a contract for real property. For instance, a buyer who decides to place a property inside their family trust after writing the initial purchase contract can assign his interest from himself as an individual to the trust.

KEY IDEAS TO REMEMBER:
- Though the buyer can assign his interest in a contract to a third party, the original buyer (or assignor) remains legally liable for completion of the contract.
- All contracts are fully assignable unless specified otherwise in the contact.

Options, First Right of Refusal & Lease Options

An **option** allows a party (the **optionee**) to purchase the right to buy a parcel of real property at a set price before a set date in exchange for valid consideration. This agreement should be recorded for the protection of the optionee. This agreement also encumbers the title to the property.

An option is a **unilateral** contract. The **optionee** is not required to exercise the option but the seller of the option, the **optionor**, is required to sell if the option is exercised.

With **first right of refusal**, a party offers valid consideration to a property owner whose property is not currently for sale. This agreement says the property owner will contact the holder of the first right of refusal first if the property is placed on the market so the holder has the first chance to either accept or reject the seller's terms. This agreement, also known as a right to preemption, should be recorded for the protection of the holder of the first right of refusal. The agreement also encumbers the property.

Lease options and **lease purchases** are both rent-to-own scenarios. On a **lease option**, the tenant has the option to purchase the property at the end of the lease. On a **lease purchase**, the tenant is obligated to purchase the property at the end of the lease.

Non-compete Agreements

A **non-compete agreement** is exactly what it sounds like – an agreement not to compete against one's employer for a set period after the employment terminates.

Chapter 6
Property Interests, Estates & Tenancies

The ideas that follow are some of real estate's foundational concepts. Many of these apply to real estate anywhere in the United States, while some will be Arizona specific. Given the importance of these basic building blocks of real estate, you can expect multiple questions in this area.

Real Property Definitions

- **Land** is the surface of the earth, down to the center of the earth and into the sky above.
- **Real estate** is the land plus everything attached, such as buildings and landscaping.
- **Real property** is the real estate plus the attached rights of ownership.

KEY IDEAS TO REMEMBER:
- Land – the ground below, the air above and all in between
- Real estate – land + improvements
- Real property – land + real estate + rights of ownership

Mineral rights and **air rights** both are part of real property. While the U.S. Government places an upper limit on air rights and mineral rights often are sold separately from the property, for our purposes, air rights and mineral rights are **appurtenant.**

Appurtenant means **"runs with the land"** and includes not just those items that are physically attached, but non-attached items that are intended to remain with the property (think of house keys or garage door openers.)

Characteristics of Land

Land has both physical and economic characteristics.

Among land's physical characteristics is that it is immovable, indestructible and non-homogenous. But, for our purposes, the most important physical characteristic of land is **situs**. Situs is the idea behind the old saying "location, location, location." Land can gain or lose value simply on the basis of where it's located. That's situs.

It's best to know all three economic characteristics of land:

- **Scarcity** – we're not making any more land. What's there is there. (Forget Dubai!)
- **Modification** – an owner can modify or improve their property as needed.
- **Fixity** – land is a fixed, or frozen, or illiquid asset. Land cannot be converted easily into cash if you needed money in a hurry, unlike stocks or money market accounts.

Real property can be **corporeal** – tangible – or **incorporeal** – intangible.

KEY IDEAS TO REMEMBER:
- A house would be considered corporeal real property because it's tangible.
- An easement or right-of-way would be incorporeal real property because it's intangible.

Fixtures and Attachments

Fixtures can be either natural or man-made. We will start with natural attachments.

Most natural attachments are called **natural fruits**. Natural fruits include anything growing on the land, whether growing naturally or planted for landscaping purposes. Natural fruits are **real property**.

The other category of natural attachments is **industrial fruits**. Industrial fruits include anything intentionally planted for commercial purposes. The basic idea between industrial fruits, also known as **crops** or **emblements** is that society should not get in the way of an individual's ability to make a living. Therefore, industrial fruits are considered **personal property**.

KEY IDEA TO REMEMBER:
- An orange tree planted in your backyard is real property. The orange trees planted in a commercial orchard is personal property.

Through the **doctrine of emblements**, a tenant farmer can return to the property one time after close of escrow to harvest his crops because they are his personal property.

KEY IDEA TO REMEMBER:
- A property is sold in April, when the corn planted for commercial purposes is only knee high. The tenant farmer can come back one time, in July when ready for harvest, because of the doctrine of emblements.

Man-made attachments are called **fixtures**. A fixture is an item of personal property attached to real property, thus turning the item into real property.

KEY IDEAS TO REMEMBER:
- Annexation is the legal term for attaching the personal property to make it real property.
- Severance is the legal term for removing the item, turning it back into personal property.

For example, if I replace a ceiling fan in my home, the fan sitting new in the box on the floor is personal property. When I install it, it becomes real property through annexation. The old fan once removed, becomes personal property again through severance.

Trade fixtures are the man-made equivalent to industrial fruits or emblements. Trade fixtures are items of personal property installed by a commercial tenant for purposes of their business. Trade fixtures remain personal property as long as they were installed by the tenant and removed before their lease expires.

KEY IDEA TO REMEMBER:
- A pizza oven installed by a tenant opening a new restaurant would be a trade fixture and is considered personal property. The tenant only would need to make sure that they remove the pizza oven prior to expiration of the lease.

Bundle of Rights

Under the **feudal system** of land ownership, all real property belonged to the king. With the signing of the Magna Carta in 1215 and the implementation of its conditions three years later, the **allodial system** was created. The allodial system created individual real property rights for the first time.

With the allodial system, an owner of real property receives certain rights. These are known collectively as the **Bundle of Rights**

- **Control** – the owner can improve their property however they wish – add a fence, add a pool, add a room, etc.
- **Disposition** – the owner can dispose of the property however they wish – sell it, give it away, rent it or otherwise encumber it.
- **Exclusion** – the owner can keep others from using their property or even stepping foot onto it.
- **Possession** – the owner has the right not just to own the property by physically possess it – live on it and make it productive.

- **Usage** (also known as enjoyment) – the owner can use their property free from interference from others or society as long as they don't interfere with anyone else's enjoyment.

There are three vocabulary terms dealing with impositions on an owner's Bundle of Rights:

- **Encroachment** – a physical object over the property line, such as a fence in the wrong place or tree branches hanging over the fence.
- **Nuisance** – anything occurring off the property interfering with an owner's usage.
- **Trespass** – a person on the owner's property without permission.

Deeds and Bills of Sale

A **deed** is the piece of paper used to transfer ownership of real property. The real property is being **granted** through the deed. Which means, the person granting or conveying title is the **grantor** and the person receiving title is the **grantee**.

KEY IDEA TO REMEMBER:
- The grantor conveys the deed to the grantee.

Personal property is transferred through a **bill of sale**. This bill of sale generally would be separate from the main contract for the property and often is handled outside of escrow.

Uniform Commercial Code

KEY IDEAS TO REMEMBER:
- The Uniform Commercial Code (UCC) is the law that regulates paperwork used to transfer personal property.
- The UCC-1 is a form used to transfer personal property in a commercial transaction. The UCC-1 in Arizona is filed with the Arizona Secretary of State.

Manufactured Homes

Manufactured homes, by definition, are **personal property**. A manufactured home does not become real property until it has permanently affixed to a parcel of real property and an **affidavit of affixture** has been issued.

KEY IDEAS TO REMEMBER:
- Manufactured homes in a mobile home park, where the owner of the manufactured home leases their space, are considered personal property.

41

- Real estate licensees in Arizona can sell either attached or unattached manufactured homes, in other words, whether the manufactured home is personal or real property.
- If the owner of an unattached manufactured home wants to abandon title to the home, he would take the title to the Motor Vehicle Division.

Real Estate Interests and Ownership

There are two overarching categories of real estate interests or **estate**. An estate is an interest in real property that, at a minimum, involves possession. It may include ownership, depending on the estate. Estates can be either **freehold** or **less than freehold**, also known as **leasehold**.

KEY IDEAS TO REMEMBER:
- A freehold estate includes both ownership and possession.
- A leasehold estate is what it sounds like – a lease – and only includes possession.

We will start first with freehold estates. Leasehold estates have their own chapter.

Fee Simple vs. Defeasible Fee

The most common, and most complete, form of estate is **fee simple** or **fee simple absolute**. The owner of a fee simple estate holds all the bundle of rights of ownership and, for all intents and purposes, can do what they wish with the property (keeping in mind the government rights we'll review soon.)

With a **defeasible** or **qualified fee estate**, a condition has been placed on the ownership by the grantor. If that condition ever is violated by the grantee, the property reverts back to the grantor with no court proceeding necessary.

Note: In some real estate classes, defeasible or qualified fee is further divided into determinable and conditional fee. For our purposes, you won't need to know the difference between the two. The main testable idea is the defeasible or qualified fee estate.

Defeasible Fee Examples

Scottsdale Airport is an example of a defeasible estate. The land was given to the city by the Seventh Day Adventist Church with the one condition that the property must be an airport. If the city ever closes the airport, ownership would revert back to the Church automatically. The city can sell the airport but, since a seller never can convey more ownership than they hold, the same condition will apply to the new buyer – the property would need to remain an airport.

One more example – the Garden of Eden. Ownership was given to Adam and Eve with one condition – don't eat the fruit. I think we know how this one worked out.

Ordinary/Conventional Life Estates

Life estates can be either **conventional** (also known as **ordinary**) and statutory. We will start with the ordinary life estates.

All ordinary life estates have three basic components:

- A **grantor**, who sets up the life estate at the beginning.
- A **grantee**, known as the life tenant, who receives conditional ownership of the property.
- A **measuring life**. Life estates are conditional estates, but the condition is a person's life span.

A life tenant can sell their life estate, rent the property, even encumber it. The only thing the life tenant cannot do is leave the property to their heirs as a fee simple estate because they don't have a fee simple estate to give.

No matter what question you encounter about ordinary or conventional life estates, there only are four possible scenarios that you will need to know. Best of all, these questions are plug and play – plug in the name of each party and your answer is revealed.

We're going to set this up, scenario by scenario.

First up is Alice and Ben. Alice has an extra house and wants to make sure Ben has a place to live for the rest of her life. She could give him the house outright, but she wants to decide what happens to the house when Ben passes away. She could let him live in the house rent free, but she still would be responsible for insurance, taxes and other liability. So, what Alice will do is set up a life estate instead.

GRANTOR	LIFE TENANT	MEASURING LIFE	REMAINDERMAN
Alice ⟶	Ben	Ben	

Under this scenario, when Ben – the measuring life – dies, the house is going to go back to Alice. We call this **reversion** and say Alice has a **future estate in reversion** or a **reversionary interest**.

GRANTOR   LIFE TENANT   MEASURING LIFE   REMAINDERMAN

Alice ⟶ Ben   Ben

REVERSION

That's scenario one. For scenario two, let's add an extra person to the mix. Let's say Alice doesn't want the house back when Ben passes. Instead, she wants to see her friend David get the house. David, as the **third party** getting the house after the death of the grantee/life tenant, is the **remainderman** and holds a **future estate in remainder**.

More specifically, David would be the **vested remainderman** because he is specifically named in the life estate to get the house when the life tenant dies.

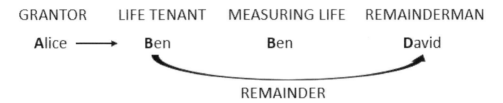

GRANTOR   LIFE TENANT   MEASURING LIFE   REMAINDERMAN

Alice ⟶ Ben   Ben   David

REMAINDER

For the third scenario, we're going to change the measuring life.

If the measuring life is **anyone other than the life tenant**, this a life estate **pur autre vie**. Pur autre vie means, literally, for the life of another. Our last two lines in the above diagram both are **life estates pur autre vie** because the measuring life is a third person, not the grantee.

One real life example of this, as one of my students shared, was a family friend who had an adult child with Downs Syndrome. His sister was caring for him, so the parents gave the house to his sister based on his lifespan – a way of giving him the house for his use, even when he was not mentally competent to take ownership traditionally.

Let's have Alice give the house to Ben, for the life of Carol.

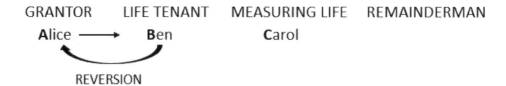

This is exactly like our first scenario, except we have substituted a third party for the measuring life, making this a life estate pur autre vie.

Lastly, let's set up a life estate pur autre vie with a remainderman:

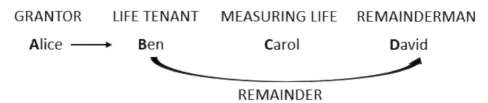

Alice is giving the house to Ben, for the life of Carol, and when Carol dies, ownership will transfer to David.

Putting all four of them together:

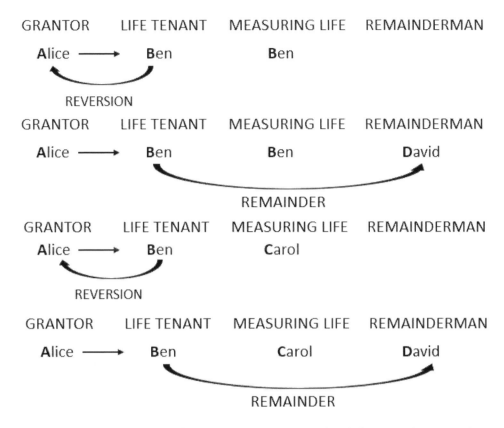

As I said at the beginning of this section, plug ang play. Substitute the names into one of those four scenarios and you can answer any question that comes up dealing with conventional life estates

KEY IDEAS TO REMEMBER:

- Ownership NEVER moves in reversion or remainder until the measuring life dies.
- Once established in reversion or remainder, the property will convey either in reversion or in remainder upon the death of the measuring **life NO MATTER WHAT**.

So, if the vested remainderman dies before the measuring life, nothing changes immediately with the ownership. But once the measuring life dies, ownership still will move in remainder but to the vested remainderman's heirs. They are referred to as **contingent remaindermen** because their ownership is contingent on the death of the vested remainderman.

And, if the grantor dies before the measuring life, again, nothing changes immediately with the ownership. But once the measuring life dies, ownership will move in reversion to the heirs of the grantor.

Lastly, if the life tenant dies before the measuring life on a life estate pur autre vie, ownership will move to the life tenant's heirs, at least until the measuring life dies.

Note: **NEVER** add extra layers to this. We don't really care if the grantor or vested remainderman has heirs because we're keeping escheat and probate and laws of descent out of this. No need to make any of this more complicated than necessary.

Homestead

Homestead is the only valid statutory life estates in Arizona. Homestead protects up to $150,000 of the equity of a homeowner's primary residence in the event of an unforeseen judgment.

KEY IDEAS TO REMEMBER:
- Homestead applies to general creditors – judgment liens – not specific creditors such as property taxes, special assessments, home loans, HOA liens, etc.
- Homestead applies only to one's primary residence, not investment or vacation homes.
- Homestead applies only to natural persons, not corporations or LLCs.
- A homeowner can have only one homestead exemption. It does not matter how many properties they own.

These are the **Arizona** homestead laws so, naturally, if the owner switches their primary residence to a property outside Arizona, homestead is lost. Homestead also is lost if the property is sold.

Easements

An **easement** is the right to use someone else's property without possessing it. An easement is a right-of-way and is considered intangible real property. It is a non-possessory interest and does not constitute an estate which, as mentioned, requires at least possession.

Appurtenant Easements

An **appurtenant easement** generally involves two parcels of real estate and is used for **ingress** and **egress** – the legal ability to enter and exit a property.

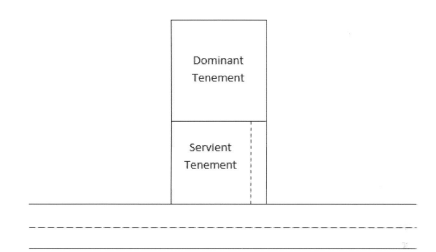

KEY IDEAS TO REMEMBER:
- The dominant tenement has the benefit of the easement.
- The servient tenement has the burden of the easement.
- The easement only can be terminated by the owner of the dominant tenement. One way to think of an appurtenant easement is in terms of value. A landlocked parcel, one that lacks legal access, has virtually no value because it can't be reached legally (except by helicopter, jet pack or a pole vault!) With an appurtenant easement, providing permanent access, the parcel suddenly has value.

KEY IDEA TO REMEMBER:
- Whenever asked about the easement needed to provide permanent access to a property, think of the value aspect and consider appurtenant easements first.

Easements in Gross

Unlike an appurtenant easement, which usually involves two parcels, an **easement in gross** is a personal easement. It constitutes a legal right of use, burdening a **servient tenement**.

Do you have a utility box in your front yard? Do you have a water meter? These are easements in gross. You own the land where the utility box sits. You pay taxes on it. But the utility company owns the right of use of that small portion of your property. The same goes for the water meter. **Like with an appurtenant easement, only the holder of the easement can terminate the easement.**

Prescriptive Easements

Prescriptive easements, also known as **easements by prescription**, are easements created through adverse possession. There are four requirements to create a prescriptive easement. The use of the property has to be **open, notorious, hostile** and **continuous.**

- Open – that the use is not being hidden.
- Notorious – that anyone paying attention would observe the property in use.
- Hostile – that the use is without the owner's permission.
- Continuous – that the use has occurred for at least 10 years.

KEY IDEAS TO REMEMBER:
- An individual's use can be less than the 10 years as long as there was adverse use in general for 10 or more. This concept is called tacking – the ability to tack on one's use onto prior use.
- To gain a prescriptive easement, the party using the property would go to court and file a prescriptive suit.
- License – permission to use the property – ends the possibility of prescription because the use no longer is hostile.

An easement by prescription only applies to the portion of a property being used. One example would be a property owner who drives over a portion of his neighbor's property to reach his own without permission. If allowed to happen for 10 years, this could result in a permanent easement being created through prescription.

We will talk more about prescription when we review adverse possession.

Easement by Necessity

Easements by necessity are court-ordered easement. This would be the last way a property owner would want to see an easement created as it requires convincing the court of the necessity of creating an easement – no small feat.

KEY IDEA TO REMEMBER:
- Easements by necessity most often are used to create legal access – ingress and egress – to an otherwise landlocked parcel.

Conservation Easements

A **conservation easement** is exactly what it sounds like – an easement purchased by a conservation group to preserve a particular habitat or area. For example, there are conservation easements in place along the San Pedro River in southeast Arizona to preserve the native beaver habitat.

View Easements

Like conservation easements, **view easements** are exactly what they sound like – easements designed to protect a view. For example, homeowners living next to golf courses or greenspaces often have view fencing in their yard – a solid bottom with wrought iron on top. The HOA holds a view easement which prevents the owner from being able to construct a full-sized solid fence, preserving the view.

License

License is another word for permission. Unlike easements, licenses often are informal and they can be revoked at any time. Think of a fishing license. The fishing license gives the holder permission to fish in state waters. It can't be transferred and it can be revoked at any time.

Types of Tenancies – How to Take Title

It's crucial for a real estate licensee to understand the different ways in which a property owner can hold title to their property. Having said that, we **NEVER** advise clients how to take title as it's a decision with legal and tax ramifications.

Sole and Separate/In Severalty

This is the most basic form of ownership. When an individual purchases property, they take ownership **sole and separate**. This also is known as **in severalty** – not severalty in terms of several owners but severalty in terms of the owner's interest being severed from anyone else.

KEY IDEA TO REMEMBER:
- When a government entity takes ownership of property, it does so in severalty.

Tenants in Common/Joint Tenancy

When two or more unmarried people purchase property in Arizona, they will take title either as **tenants in common** or **joint tenancy**.

Tenants in common allows each owner to leave their share to their heirs. That means the property will have to go through probate when an owner dies. Also, tenants in common is the only tenancy in which owners can have unequal shares.

KEY IDEA TO REMEMBER:

- If two or more unmarried people buy property in Arizona, their ownership will default to tenants in common unless they take other action. So, when asked about the type of tenancy held when two unmarried people buy property and you know nothing else of the transaction, the answer is tenants in common.

Joint tenancy also involves two or more unmarried people. But unlike tenants in common, joint tenancy always has **rights of survivorship (you may see this as JTRoS)**. This means when one joint tenant dies, her share of the property will be distributed among the surviving joint tenants **without probate**.

There are **four unities** that have to exist for joint tenancy to take place:

- **Unity of time**– everyone bought at the same time
- **Unity of title**– there is just one deed
- **Unity of interest**– each joint tenant has undivided interest
- **Unity of possession**– each joint tenant has undivided possession

Without any of the four unities, joint tenancy is not possible.

KEY IDEA TO REMEMBER:

- A joint tenant's will NEVER can override the rights of survivorship. The will is irrelevant.

Rights of Survivorship

Rights of survivorship can be confusing. When most of us hear "survivor," we think of surviving heirs. But that's not the case with rights of survivorship in real property ownership.

Think of rights of survivorship as a life raft. Four people buy property together as joint tenants with rights of survivorship, so we place all four of them in the life raft. If one dies, the others will distribute the deceased's assets equally (after rifling through his pockets), then throw him over the side for the sharks to eat.

Harsh? Of course. But the point is, the outside world is irrelevant when you're in a life raft.

KEY IDEA TO REMEMBER:

- The last surviving joint tenant now owns the property in severalty and can leave it to their heirs, etc. because there are no other joint tenants to share ownership.

Let's look at an example. Four gentlemen buy property together:

George	John	Thomas	James
25%	25%	25%	25%

Now, one of them passes away. Sorry, President Washington …

George	John	Thomas	James
R.I.P.	33%	33%	33%

George's shares automatically transfer to the surviving joint tenancies. **No probate** is required because the transfer is automatic. George's will would be irrelevant.

Adams died a few hours ahead of Jefferson, so …

George	John	Thomas	James
R.I.P.	R.I.P.	50%	50%

Then, once Jefferson passed away …

George	John	Thomas	James
R.I.P.	R.I.P.	R.I.P.	100%

As the last surviving joint tenant, Madison now owns the property in severalty.

KEY IDEA TO REMEMBER:
- There only is ONE kind of joint tenancy and it ALWAYS involves rights of survivorship.
- To terminate a joint tenancy, the owners would go to court and file a partition action.
- Each joint tenant can sell their share without permission of the others. The new owner takes ownership as a tenant in common. The joint tenancy remains unchanged (unless there only were two owners total, which makes the ownership tenants in common in general).

Community Property

When a married couple purchases property, they will take title as **community property**. Note: while it's possible for a married couple to take title as joint tenants or tenants in common in real life, for purposes of the test, stick to community property always.

Community property can come **with** or **without** rights of survivorship. The default for married couples in Arizona is community property **without** rights of survivorship, usually shortened to community property.

Community property without rights of survivorship requires probate because each spouse can leave their share to whomever they wish. Community property with rights of survivorship, which you may see as CPRoS, does not require probate because ownership transfers automatically.

Investment/Business Entities

You could be asked about different types of investment or business entities. The most common are **sole proprietorships, corporations, limited liability companies, syndicates** and **real estate investment trusts** or **REITs**.

Sole Proprietorship

This is the simplest way to organize a business. When you get your real estate license and activate that license with an employing broker, congratulations, you're a sole proprietorship.

KEY IDEAS TO REMEMBER:
- Sole proprietorships' profits and losses are taxed on the owner's individual tax return.
- The owner of a sole proprietorship has unlimited personal liability if sued.

Limited Liability Company

To defer liability, many business owners prefer to set up a **limited liability company (LLC)**. Profits and losses still are reflected on the owner's individual tax return, but much of the liability is shifted from the owner to the LLC.

KEY IDEAS TO REMEMBER:
- To establish an LLC, articles of organization need to be filed with the Arizona Corporation Commission.
- Real estate licensees, since they are working under an existing entity, would need to form a Professional Limited Liability Company – a PLLC – again through the corporation commission.

Corporations

There are two types of corporations you need to know – a **C Corp** and an **S Corp**. Both are created by filing articles of incorporation with the Arizona Corporation Commission. The primary difference you need to know between the two is in how they are taxed.

KEY IDEAS TO REMEMBER:
- C corporations are subject to double taxation. Profits are taxed once at the corporate level, then a second time on the shareholder level once paid as dividends.
- S corporations only have single taxation – there is no taxation at the corporate level. However, an S Corp can have no more than 100 shareholders and all must be American – foreign investment is not permitted.
- Corporations are legal persons – legal entities – that can enter contracts, sue and be sued, etc.

Real Estate Investment Trusts

A **real estate investment trust** is an investment entity similar to a mutual fund. A REIT provides instant diversification because it invests in many, many different properties. A REIT features single taxation – all taxes are paid on the shareholder level. A REIT also provides continuing operations and professional management. A REIT must have 100 or more shareholders.

REITs and corporations feature something called **passive investors**. Passive investors provide capital and their liability generally is limited to what they invest. Passive investors do not have any decision-making authority.

KEY IDEA TO REMEMBER:
- Passive investment can best be remembered as "give me your money, sit down, shut up and hold on."

Co-ops, Condos and Timeshares … Oh My!

Cooperative

A **cooperative** is a particular type of common ownership in which a building is owner be a corporation and those purchasing into the co-op are buying shares of the corporation, NOT real property. "Owners" in a co-op take possession through a **long-term proprietary lease** and are governed by the **Arizona Landlord-Tenant Act**.

Co-op shareholders pay an annual assessment for taxes, insurance and, if appropriate, the mortgage for the property.

KEY IDEA TO REMEMBER:
- The assessments must be paid in full by the shareholders. So, if there are vacancies or others are nor paying, everyone else will make a larger appointment to cover the shortfall.

Condominium

A **condominium** is a form of common ownership where the owner will have **fee simple** ownership of their unit and an undivided interest in the common areas as **tenants in common**. Condo owners have **horizontal rights** – they own generally from the drywall in. They do not have individual ownership rights to anything above or below their unit. Unit ownership also can be referred to as an **air lot** or **cubage**.

Condominiums are created through a **master deed**, which divides the property into the individual units for purchase. **Condo conversions** are apartments that have been converted into condominiums.

Note: While you may have discussed townhouses in your licensing classes, these are not really tested. The only difference of note between condos and townhouses is that the latter comes with vertical rights. There are other minor differences but, again, these generally are not testable subjects.

Planned Unit Development

A **planned unit development** is a project where detailed zoning has been created, either conforming to or amending a municipality's larger zoning plans. A PUD usually includes not just residential, but also commercial and other retail uses.

Timeshares

A **timeshare** is another version of common ownership. With a timeshare, buyers are taking title **tenants in common**. But rather than dividing ownership on the property itself, the tenants in common refers to the different intervals of time buyers purchase. There are a handful of things to know on timeshares:

KEY IDEAS TO REMEMBER:
- Owners purchase real property but only for certain intervals of time. Thus, time shares also are known as interval ownership.

- A real estate license is needed to sell time shares, but not for the telemarketing calls. Those telemarketers must be supervised by a designated broker while calling.
- Time shares often give gifts for sitting through the presentation. What to know:
    - The gift must be disclosed before the presentation.
    - The presentation can be no more than 120 minutes.
    - The gift must be given immediately following the presentation.
- Buyers of a time share have a seven-calendar day rescission period.

Chapter 7
Government Rights

In the previous chapter, we talked about the individual ownership rights of real property – the bundle of rights, air rights, mineral rights, hereditaments, etc. Now we are going to focus on the rights reserved by the government.

There are four government rights, which are most easily remembered through the mnemonic PETE:

- **Police power**
- **Eminent domain**
- **Taxation**
- **Escheat**

Each of these is a separate right. Be careful to not make the common mistake as confusing the phrase "police power" with all four government rights as a whole. Police power is only one of the four rights.

Police Power

Police power deals with anything created through legislation. This includes everything from real estate licensing laws to subdivision regulations to zoning ordinances. The Arizona Legislature passes statutes as a part of police power. One type of statute, **enabling acts**, empowers municipalities to pass their own **ordinances**.

Wetlands, water-based ecological systems protected by statute, are protected through police power.

The most commonly tested police power is **zoning**, which we will cover in another chapter.

Eminent Domain

Eminent domain is the government's right to take private property for public use. Eminent domain only applies to real property, not personal property. To take private property through eminent domain, the government files a lawsuit called a **condemnation** action. Once taken, the government owes the prior owner **just or fair compensation**.

KEY IDEAS TO REMEMBER:
- Eminent domain requires two things:
  - o Due process through the condemnation action
  - o Just or fair compensation to the property owner
- Eminent domain is the government's **RIGHT**. The **ACTION** is condemnation. Make sure to read questions on eminent domain/condemnation carefully to determine what the test wants.

Taxation

Taxation, as I'm sure you already know, is the government's way of raising revenue to fund itself. In Arizona, the main source of tax revenue are **property taxes**. Real property in Arizona is taxed on an **ad valorem** basis. Ad valorem means according to value, so real property in Arizona s taxed according to its **assessed value**.

Property Tax Basics

First, the county assessor determines the "market" value of the property. I put market in quotes because the assessor's "market" value usually is different than a property's value in the open market. The market value is determined one of two ways:

- **Full cash value.** This is an approximation of actual market value. In practical terms, the full cash value usually is lower than the property's open market value.
- **Limited Property Value** – LPV is determined through a statutory formula and cannot exceed the full cash value. This is what has been used almost exclusively as market value since 2015.

Next, the assessor's market value is multiplied by a statutorily-set assessment ratio. Properties are assessed and classified annually at the first of the year. Different types of properties are assessed at different percentages of market value:

- **Commercial (Class 1) – 18 percent**
- **Vacant land (Class 2) – 15 percent**
- **Residential (Class 3) – 10 percent**
- **Residential rental (Class 4) – 10 percent**

An existing property would be taxed according to its classification on January 1. A new build, for example, would be assessed as vacant land the year it was sold, then be re-assessed as residential property the following January.

The assessor then will take this assessed value and multiply it by a taxing jurisdiction's tax rate (the jurisdiction's tax budget divided by the assessed value of all the jurisdiction's real property). For example, a jurisdiction with a budget of $1 million and assessed value of $20 million would have a 5 percent tax rate. (1,000,000 divided by 20,000,000).

Let's put this together ...

> **Q: A residential property in Phoenix has an LPV of $250,000. Phoenix has a tax rate of 4 percent. What is the property owner's tax bill?**
>
> **A: $1,000. ($250,000 x 10% assessment ratio = $25,000. $25,000 x 4% tax rate = $1,000)**

KEY IDEA TO REMEMBER:
- Tax rates are expressed in terms of dollars per $100 of assessed value. So, a tax rate of 4 percent, would be stated as $4 per $100 of assessed value. Having said that, for the math, just multiply the percentage and the assessed value. It's far easier this way.

Property owners can appeal the valuation of their property through the county.

Property Tax Liens

Property taxes in Arizona are assessed as of January 1. Property taxes in Arizona are paid **in arrears**. Because of this, the county places a **tax lien** on real property as of the **first Monday in January**.

KEY IDEA TO REMEMBER:
- A lien is a financial encumbrance, a way for a creditor to make sure they are paid.

Property taxes in Arizona are assessed annually but **paid semi-annually**. First half taxes are due **October 1**, late **November** 1. Second half taxes are due **March 1**, late **May 1**. All tax payments are made to the **county treasurer**. Here's the timeline you will need to know.

If taxes are not paid on time, they are subject to a **16% annual penalty**. The tax lien also can be subject to a **tax lien sale**.

KEY IDEAS TO REMEMBER:

- Tax lien sales are held in February (each county has a different date).
- The sales are sold at a reverse auction. Bidding starts at the 16% penalty rate and decreases from there.
- The winner is whomever bids the lowest rate of interest. They pay the delinquent taxes (no penalty), become the new lien holder and receive a Certificate of Sale.
- The winner **DOES NOT** receive the deed. They receive a **certificate of purchase**.
- The property owner has a three-year redemption period during which they can redeem the tax lien by paying the county the back taxes plus the full 16% annual penalty.
    - o If the taxes are redeemed, the county keeps the difference between the 16% and the winning bid interest rate. The winner of the Certificate of Purchase gets their bid rate.
- At the end of the three years, the holder of the Certificate of Sale can file a foreclosure action and then would receive a Treasurer's Deed.
- The lienholder (holder of the Certificate of Sale) can extend the redemption period.
- If no one bids at the auction, anyone can go to the treasurer's office and purchase the lien.

Special Assessments

Special assessments are particular taxes paid by property owners who receive a specific improvement. For instance, a municipality may levy a special assessment to pay for streets to be paved, sidewalks to be installed, sewer lines to be extended, etc. Those property owners who benefit from the improvement, for example, the owner whose home now has a sidewalk in front of it, pay the assessment.

Special assessments are **pro rata** – according to benefit received. They generally are assessed based on the **front footage** of the property– usually the front of the lot.

Lien Priority

Liens have a priority order of redemption:

1. **Property Taxes**
2. **Special Assessments**
3. **Mechanic's Liens**

4. **Mortgage/Deed of Trust**
   a. **HOA**
5. **Judgments**
6. **IRS**

When a property is transferred, the first lien to be satisfied is property taxes, followed by special assessments, etc. Property taxes always are in first or **superior** lien position.

Technically, judgments and the IRS are in the same bucket but, on the test, it sometimes helps to look for the IRS in an answer.

Property tax liens also are special liens – attaching to a specific piece of real property only. They are involuntary or statutory liens – derived through statute. And they do not need to be recorded to be valid, unlike other liens.

HOA Foreclosure

Just like property owners can lose their property for failure to pay property taxes, they also can lose their property for failure to pay their HOA fees.

KEY IDEA TO REMEMBER:

- HOAs in Arizona can foreclose if the property owner either owes the HOA $1,200 in fees (not including fines) or is 12 months delinquent on his HOA payments.

Chapter 8
Income Tax Aspects of Real Estate

This is one area of the curriculum that is extremely lightly tested. Having said that, there are a handful of very basic concepts you will want to know.

Types of Income
Ordinary income consists of wages, commissions, tips, interests, dividend and the like. **Capital gains** are the income generated through the sale of an asset.

Here's how you calculate capital gains for real estate:

- Start with the purchase price. This is the **basis**.
- Add the cost of improvements. This is the **adjusted basis**.
- Take the sales price. This is the **sales price**. (Redundant, I know.)
- Subtract the costs of the sale (commissions/closing costs). This is the **adjusted sales price.**
- **Subtract** the **adjusted basis** from the **adjusted sales price**. The difference is the capital gain.

Capital gains can be long-term or short-term. **Short-term capital gains** are for any asset held for 12 months or less and are taxed at ordinary tax rates. **Long-term capital gains** are for any asset held for more than 12 months and are taxed on a special schedule.

Capital Gains on Principal Residence
Selling a house normally would trigger capital gains (unless you lost money on the sale). But there are **capital gains exclusions** available to those who sell their **principal residence**.

KEY IDEAS TO REMEMBER:
- A principal residence is one in which the home owner has lived as a primary residence for at least two of the last five years.
- The exclusion is $250,000 for single taxpayers, $500,000 for married taxpayers.

- The minimum holding period is two years. For example, this deduction is available five times in a 10-year period.

The taxpayer doesn't have to be living in the house at the time of sale to be eligible. However, if the property has been turned into a rental, the exclusion is lost.

Real Estate Tax Deductions

Both **property taxes** and **mortgage interest** are deductible for those who itemize their taxes. Property owners can deduct up to $10,000 in property taxes and their full mortgage interest.

Investment Real Estate

Since investing in real estate is considered a business, many of the common expenses involved with owning a property are tax deductible.

Depreciation

Depreciation is a tax deduction that reflects the wear and tear on real estate improvements (i.e., the buildings themselves).

The most common type of depreciation is **straight line depreciation**, where the property owner deducts the same percentage of the purchase price every year for a number of years.

KEY IDEAS TO REMEMBER:
- Land never can be depreciated, only the improvements to the land.
- Statutory depreciation periods are 27 ½ years for residential, 39 years for commercial.
- Age of the property is irrelevant. The same property can be depreciated over and over again by different investors each time it's purchased.

Through **depreciation recapture**, when the property is sold, the total depreciation taken is deducted from the adjusted basis.

Tax Deferred/1031 Exchanges

Investors are able to defer capital gains taxes through a **tax deferred** or **1031 exchange**. In short, the investor is substituting one investment property for another. There are strict rules surrounding 1031 exchanges:

KEY IDEAS TO REMEMBER:

- Property has to be like-for-like. This just means real property in the United States exchanged for real property in the United States.
- The property purchased has to cost at least as much as the proceeds from the property sold.
- Every cent from the sale has to be used in the purchase.
- Investors need to identify the property they are going to be within 45 days of the close of escrow on their sale. They need to close escrow on the purchase within 180 days of COE.
- If there's a disparity in price (in other words, the investor is buying something more expensive than the proceeds), boot is added.
- Boot is the non-like kind of an exchange. It can be borrowed and it is taxable.

For our purposes, there's no need to know the whys and wherefores surrounding boot being taxed. Just know that it is taxable and move on.

Employee vs. Independent Contractor

The vast majority of real estate licensees work as **independent contractors**. If you're being paid solely on commissions, no taxes are being deducted and your broker can't tell you where to be or when to be there, you're an independent contractor and will receive a 1099 at year's end.

If the above don't apply (for example, you are working for a property manager or a builder), you are considered an **employee** and will receive a W-2.

Chapter 9
Arizona Water Law

Water law can be incredibly complicated and not just in Arizona. Fortunately, the basics needed for the test are straight forward. The basic concept to remember is that, in Arizona, the state controls virtually every drop of water not sitting in a plastic bottle next to you. The department in charge of water is the **Arizona Department of Water Resources**.

Sources of Water

There are two sources of water in Arizona. There is **groundwater**, which is in the ground. And then there is **surface water**, which is on the surface. Yes, it's that easy to remember.

Each type of water has its own governing laws.

Surface Water Law

In Arizona, surface water law is summed up in the **doctrine of prior appropriation – "first in time, first in right."** In other words, the first person to put surface water to a beneficial use has the continued right of use.

In other parts of the country, there are **riparian** and **littoral** rights for surface water. For these, just match the first letters:

- Riparian rights are for rivers and streams (Riparian/River)
- Littoral rights are for lakes and oceans (Littoral/Lake)

Ownership of land next to surface water depends on whether the waterway is considered **navigable** or **non-navigable**. A navigable waterway is one large enough to handle commercial traffic. The only navigable waterway in Arizona is the Colorado River.

KEY IDEAS TO REMEMBER:
- Homeowners next to a navigable waterway own to the average high-water mark.
- Homeowners next to a non-navigable waterway own to the average low-water mark.

Groundwater Law

Groundwater in Arizona is governed through the **Arizona Groundwater Act of 1980**. The purpose of the Groundwater Act was to end the overdraft – using more than we replenish – of groundwater in the state's most highly populated areas.

The Groundwater Act created **Active Management Areas (AMA)**, Open Areas and **Irrigation Non-Expansion Areas (INA)**.

Active Management Areas

There are five active management areas in Arizona – Prescott, Maricopa, Pinal, Pima and Santa Cruz. These areas each were identified in 1980 as suffering from a severe overdraft of ground water. The goal for these areas is a **safe yield**. We don't have to replace more groundwater than we use, but we can't use more than we replace. In other words, there needs to be a balance.

Developers wanting to build in an AMA must demonstrate they have a **100-year assured water supply**. If the developer cannot prove access to that 100-year assured water supply, they cannot build.

Open Areas

Those parts of the state not in an AMA are considered Open Areas. In the Open Areas, developers must show access to an **adequate water supply** – no time frame attached. Developers can build without this adequate water supply but have to disclose in all marketing that no water is available.

Irrigation Non-Expansion Areas

There are three irrigation non-expansion areas in Arizona – Douglas, Harquahala and Joseph City. There are no conservation measures in place, but the amount of irrigated acreage cannot be expanded.

KEY IDEAS TO REMEMBER:
- Active Management Areas – 100-year assured water supply program
- Open Areas – adequate water supply program, no timeframe
- Irrigated acreage – two acres or more used for agricultural purposes (no lawn or golf courses).

Exempt Domestic Well

Exempt domestic wells are wells accessing groundwater for non-irrigation purposes. While there are a number of details about these wells, the main idea for our purpose is this definition:

- An exempt domestic well has a maximum pump capacity of 35 gallons per minute.

All wells are registered with the Department of Water Resources and transfer paperwork must be filed when they are sold.

Grandfathered Groundwater Rights

When the Groundwater Act was passed, the Legislature looked at historic groundwater usage for the five-year period prior (1975 to 1980) and created certain grandfathered groundwater rights. Like all else with water, the details can be complicated. But for our purposes, there only are a handful of things you will need to know.

There are three grandfathered groundwater rights – **Grandfathered Irrigation**, **Non-Irrigation Type 1** and **Non-Irrigation Type 2** rights.

KEY IDEAS TO REMEMBER:
- Both Grandfathered Irrigation and Non-Irrigation Type 1 rights are appurtenant. They run with the land and cannot be sold separately from the land.
- Non-Irrigation Type 2 rights are NOT appurtenant and CAN be sold separately.

Other Water Concepts

There are a number of parties that use water in Arizona – agriculture, industrial, domestic, municipal and special users such as golf courses, residential lakes, etc.

We also have some renewable sources of water including **effluent**, which is recharged sewage.

Central Arizona Project (CAP)

The **Central Arizona Project** is an aqueduct carrying water from the Colorado River to Maricopa, Pinal and Pima counties. Arizona shares allocations from the Colorado with California and Nevada.

While some of this water is put to immediate use, much of it is recharged into our aquifers. The **Arizona Water Banking Authority** is responsible for storing water underground, "banking" it in case of drought.

Central Arizona Groundwater Replenishment District

Homeowners in a **Central Arizona Groundwater Replenishment District (CAGRD)** pay an annual assessment for the groundwater they use. It appears on their annual tax bill.

Adjudicated Water

Arizona is involved in a number of adjudicated water cases with the state's Native American tribes regarding their water claims. No need to memorize the details of the mammoth policy paper on the ADWR website. Here's what you need:

- Water adjudications are taking place ONLY on the Gila and Little Colorado River systems.
- Property owners need to file a claim to join the adjudication. Purchasing in these areas does not automatically add a property owner to the existing adjudications.

Chapter 10
Environmental Law

Environmental issues are one of the main components of disclosure by a seller and the seller's agent. There are requirements that must be followed on both the federal and state level.

Regulatory Agencies

The **Environmental Protection Agency** is the federal agency charged with maintaining the quality of the nation's air, land and water. On the state level, the **Arizona Department of Environmental Quality** has the same responsibility.

Superfund/WQARF

CERCLA, the Comprehensive Environmental Response, Compensation and Liability Act, created the **Superfund**. The Superfund is a federal pool of money used to remediate sites that have suffered from toxic contamination. These sites are on the **National Priorities List**.

On the state level, ADEQ manages the **Water Quality Assurance Revolving Fund (WQARF)**, which also is used to remediate toxic waste sites.

KEY IDEAS TO REMEMBER:
- If a property is on or in the vicinity of a Superfund/WQARF site, this is a material fact that must be disclosed.
- Generally speaking, liability for the contamination falls on the original property owner and/or any other party that contributed to the contamination. Current owners who performed the necessary environmental due diligence when purchasing generally are not liable.

Underground Storage Tanks

All **underground storage tanks** must be registered with ADEQ. Because this registration requirement was not always in place, buyers should perform due diligence to determine if there may be unknown underground storage tanks on the property so they are not hit with an expensive remediation.

Due Diligence

There are four levels to environmental due diligence. Phase I involves reviewing records for the property going back 50 years to see if there are red flags. If there are, Phase II involves testing to confirm if there is contamination. If there is, Phase III is remediation and Phase IV is ongoing maintenance.

Disclosure Issues

There are a number of environmental issues on or around a property that constitute material facts and would need to be disclosed by the seller and/or seller's agent.

- **Mold** – mold usually can be found where there was been moisture intrusion. Mold also usually needs a dark area with limited ventilation to grow.
- **Radon** – radon is an odorless, colorless gas that comes from the radioactive decay of rocks and soil.
- **Asbestos** – asbestos is a fibrous, flame-retardant, heat-resistant material that can cause various respiratory issues when disturbed. The key word with asbestos is **friable** – it crumbles easily. Asbestos can either be remediated or encapsulated, depending on circumstance.
- **Lead based paint** – sellers, on any residential property built before 1978, need to provide buyers with a **lead-based paint disclosure** and an **EPA-approved booklet** about lead based paint in the home.
  - o The above requirement ONLY applies to residential property.
- **Sick building syndrome** – people feel ill when they are in a particular building and feel better when they leave, though there is no specific cause or symptoms. I often joked that the rooms in which I taught had SBS because the students felt much better when they left!
- **Pesticides** – we all know what pesticides are. Pesticide usage in Arizona is handled by the Office of Pest Management and use of pesticides, including crop dusting, is a material fact that would need to be disclosed.
- **Wood destroying insects** – termites, carpenter ants and other wood-destroying organisms are another disclosure item. Termite inspections are not required in general, though **some lenders** will require a termite inspection before funding a loan.
- **Flood hazard** – if a property is in a designated flood zone – an area where there is a 1 in 100 chance of a regional flood taking place – this must be disclosed. **Lenders** may require buyers of properties in a flood zone to purchase **flood**

insurance. Flood maps can be found on both county and Federal Emergency Management Agency (FEMA) websites.

- o **Flood insurance** is provided through the **National Flood Insurance Program.**
- o An **elevation certificate** defines a building's elevation.

- **Expansive soils –** parts of Arizona have expansive soils. This is soil with clay-like tendencies that can absorb water and expand then retract again, causing foundation and other issues. Again, this is a material fact that must be disclosed.
- **Earth fissures –** some parts of Arizona, particularly Queen Creek/San Tan Valley and northwest Surprise in the Phoenix area, are prone to earth fissures – cracks that open in the ground. If a property is in such an area, it must be disclosed.
  - o The Arizona Geological Survey maintains maps of areas subject to fissures.
  - o Like more disclosure issues, the key concept is if the seller was aware. If the seller was not aware of fissures and the area did not appear on any map, a buyer who finds a fissure three years later can't go back and sue the seller.
- **Airports –** if a property is in the vicinity of an airport, particularly a military airport, this needs to be disclosed.

Alternative Waste Water Systems
Sellers are required to disclose to buyers whether their property is connected to a municipal **sewer** system or is using a **septic** or other **alternative system**.

KEY IDEAS TO REMEMBER:
- A septic system has to be inspected within six months BEFORE the close of escrow. This is the SELLER'S responsibility.
- Ownership transfer paperwork needs to be filed with ADEQ by the BUYER within 15 days AFTER the close of escrow.
- Percolation tests are used to determine if the ground is suitable for a septic system.

Chapter 11
Legal Land Descriptions

Legal land descriptions are required on nearly all real estate-related documents. A proper legal land description is a description detailed enough that a **surveyor could locate that one parcel separate from any other in the country**. Whether it is being used on a deed, mortgage, deed of trust or easement, the legal description is an important part of real estate.

There are three methods of legal land descriptions – **metes and bounds, lot and block** and **rectangular survey.**

Metes and Bounds

A **metes and bounds** description describes the exterior of a parcel. It always starts and ends at a **point of beginning**. From this point of beginning, the surveyor would move in a given compass direction **an arc or angle** to another point, known as a **monument, marker, pin** or stake. Then the surveyor moves in another arc or angle, then another, until returning to the **point of beginning** closing the parcel.

Metes and bounds is the **oldest system of legal descriptions** in use and creates the **longest legal descriptions**.

> *Starting at the northeast corner of 59th Avenue and Bell Road, go north 700 feet, then east 1000 feet, then south 700 feet and then back to the point of beginning*

Lot and Block

Lot and block is the method used inside subdivisions, also known as platted property. The property survey creates a **plat map**, which will include street names (if possible), lot dimensions, lot numbers, easements, etc. What you never will see on map is the alignment of the houses themselves, since are irrelevant to the planning process. You also won't monuments or markers as those belong to the rectangular survey.

 a plat these see

Rectangular Survey

The **rectangular survey system** has been in place since the late 1700s and was used in the United States for nearly all territory acquired through the Northwest Ordinance, Louisiana Purchase and the entire Southwest. The only places where this isn't used is the original colonies, Maine, Kentucky, Tennessee and Texas.

Some states share a rectangular survey. Arizona does not. The rectangular survey used in Arizona encompasses the entire state.

Gila and Salt River Baseline and Meridian (G&SRB&M)

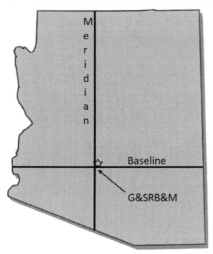

Arizona's rectangular survey is centered on the **confluence of the Gila and Salt Rivers**. The actual market is just to the east of Phoenix International Raceway on Monument Hill. From this point, two imaginary lines run across the state. The line running north and south is the **principal meridian**. The line running east and west is the **principal baseline**. And yes, Baseline Road runs along the baseline.

Because of the starting point, our rectangular survey is known as the **Gila and Salt River Baseline and Meridian**.

Township Lines and Range Lines, Tiers and Ranges

From these two primary lines, we are going to build a grid system. Every six miles, parallel to the baseline, are lines running east and west called **township lines**. And, every six miles, parallel to the meridian, are lines running north and south called **range lines**.

These sets of parallel lines create **six mile by six mile squares** called **townships**.

KEY IDEA TO REMEMBER:
- Townships are six miles on each side. This makes a township both 36 square miles and six miles square. Square miles describes the area, miles square is the length of one leg of a square.

Tiers and Ranges

Now, think of the grid you see to the side as a spreadsheet with rows and columns.

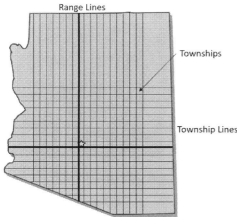

Each **horizontal row** of townships is called a tier.

Each **vertical row** of townships is called a range.

Individual townships are identified by the tier and range in which they are located. And these tiers and ranges are labeled according to their distance either north or south (for tiers) or east or west (for ranges) from the principal baseline and principal meridian.

In other words, that first column to the right (east) of the meridian is Range 1 East, followed by Range 2 E, R3E, R4E and so on.

The first row above (north) of the baseline is Tier 1 North, followed by Tier 2 N, T3N, T4N and so on.

Townships

To make this easier, let's expand the map so we're looking at a smaller area and not the entire state of Arizona at once.

You could be asked the distance from one township to either the baseline or the meridian, or even from the G&SRB&M (the center point on the grid) itself. All you need to do is remember township and range lines are six miles apart, then count by sixes. Unless you're given a specific side of the township, your answer will include two numbers – the closest and farthest corners of the township.

Looking at the diagram on the next page, let's take a look at township T4N R4E. (When describing a township, the tier always comes first). If you were asked the distance from this township to the baseline, simply start at the baseline and count your way up, six miles per line.

The answer would be 18-24 miles – 18 to the closest corner, 24 to the farthest.

R6W	R5W	R4W	R3W	R2W	R1W	R1E	R2E	R3E	R4E	R5E	R6E	
												T6N
												T5N
								24				T4N
								18				T3N
								12				T2N
								6				T1N
												T1S
												T2S
												T3S
												T4S
												T5S
												T6S

If the question was the distance from the meridian, do the same thing – start at the meridian and count the lines, six miles per line. The answer again is 18 to 24 miles.

Government Check

What happens when you place a two-dimensional grid over a three-dimensional globe? The grid stretches and gets distorted because of the curve of the globe. Since the idea of the rectangular survey is to keep everything as uniform as possible, we need to account for that stretching. This is where we use a **government check**.

A government check takes place every 24 miles – every four townships – and creates a 24-mile by 24-mile block. Every 24 miles, we adjust the boundaries of the township to account for the curvature of the earth. In the Phoenix area's East Valley, we see this on several streets which jog to the west before interesting with baseline road.

KEY IDEAS TO REMEMBER:
- Government checks take place every 24 miles, every four townships
- There are 16 townships in a government check

In creating townships, we have taken the state of Arizona and divided into 36 square mile parcels. But to identify a particular parcel, we need to go smaller. This is where we move into sections.

Sections

All townships are divided into 36 sections. Remember, a township is 36 square miles. So, if there are 36 sections, each section must be one square mile.

KEY IDEAS TO REMEMBER:
- Sections are one mile by one mile squares, so they are both one square mile in area and one mile square (length of the leg of a square).
- Sections contain 640 acres. Again – each section has 640 acres.

6	5	4	3	2	1
7	8	9	10	11	12
18	17	16	15	14	13
19	20	21	22	23	24
30	29	28	27	26	25
31	32	33	34	35	36

All sections are numbered the same. **Section 1 always is the northeast corner** and we move west from there. Then we zig-zag back. Think about it – these sections were laid out by a guy on a horse, so at every edge he had to turn the horse around and go back the other way.

When you get into the testing room, draw the section diagram you see here – almost every question dealing with sections can be answered just by using this diagram.

Fractional Sections

We just discussed government checks and how these adjustments in the borders of a township account for the curvature of the earth. Logic says that if we are adjusting the borders of the township, we also have to be adjusting the borders of the sections within that township. We do this with **fractional** or **non-standard sections**.

Fractional sections always are on the **north west** edges of a township. The idea, again, is consistency.

6	5	4	3	2	1
7	8	9	10	11	12
18	17	16	15	14	13
19	20	21	22	23	24
30	29	28	27	26	25

and

You could be asked how many fractional sections there are in each township. There are 11 – sections 1 through 6, then 7, 18, 19, 30 and 31. You also can be asked which section of four is a fractional. It will be one of the ones I just listed and that are in gray to the left. This also means there are **25 standard sections**.

Make sure you use the diagram on these questions. On the first question, there likely will be answer of 12 fractional sections in hopes a student will think there are six sections on the northern edge, six on the west, forgetting that they just counted section six twice. Make sense?

Distance Between Sections

If you get a question about the distance between sections, **always start at the corner of the section closest to the other section in the question.** just count the lines, one mile per line. **NEVER diagonally**. As one student once put it, use Uber directions – straight lines, street by street.

For example, if you were asked the distance between section 2 and section 32, we will use the corners closest to each other.

6	5	4	3	2	1
7	8	9	10	11	12
18	17	16	15	14	13
19	20	21	22	23	24
30	29	28	27	26	25
31	32	33	34	35	36

Then travel

Count one mile per line and you should end up with an answer of **six miles**.

One variation on this question is when you are given specific corners of the townships. Again, using section 2 section 32, let's change the question to ask the distance the northeast corner of section 2 to the southwest of section 32.

6	5	4	3	2	1
7	8	9	10	11	12
18	17	16	15	14	13
19	20	21	22	23	24
30	29	28	27	26	25
31	32	33	34	35	36

and from corner

Count the lines, one mile per, and you should end up with an answer of **10 miles**.

Contiguous and Abutting Sections

Contiguous sections touch at any point while **abutting sections** share one full border. If you think of the Four Corners states, Arizona is contiguous to Utah, Colorado and New Mexico but abutting only Utah or New Mexico.

Greg	Mike	Marsha Marsha Marsha
Peter	Alice	Jan
Bobby	Carol	Cindy

Or, for another example, think about the Brady family. (If you don't know who the Bradys are, I might suggest a Hulu subscription)!

All of the Bradys are contiguous the Alice because all of their squares touch her square at some point. But only Mike, Peter, Jan and Carol are abutting Alice's square because only those share a full border.

Questions about contiguous or abutting sections are testing two concepts – **does the student know how to draw the section diagram** and **does the student understand one township is surrounded by other townships**.

If asked what sections are contiguous or abutting a given section, always remember the answer will contain **one section from the township you're in** and one **section from one of the three neighboring townships**.

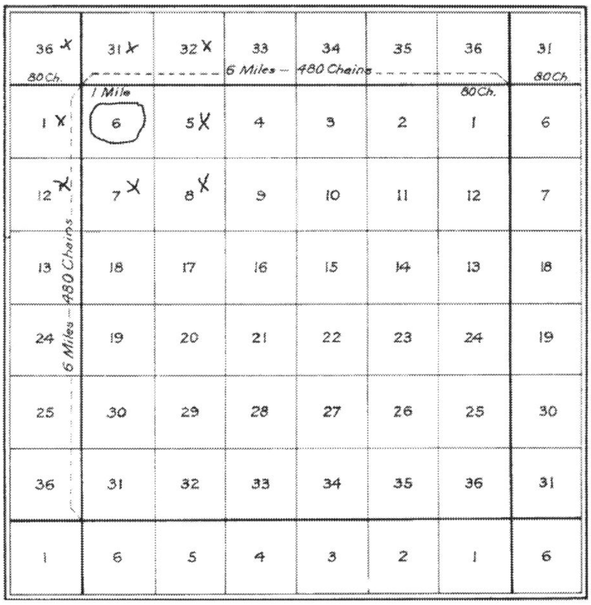
36 ✗ 31 ✗ 32 ✗ 33 34 35 36 31
80 Ch.
6 Miles – 480 Chains
80 Ch.
1 Mile
80 Ch.
1 ✗ 6 5 ✗ 4 3 2 1 6
12 ✗ 7 ✗ 8 ✗ 9 10 11 12 7
13 18 17 16 15 14 13 18
24 19 20 21 22 23 24 19
25 30 29 28 27 26 25 30
36 31 32 33 34 35 36 31
1 6 5 4 3 2 1 6
6 Miles – 480 Chains

Take, for example, section 6 from the diagram to the left. This diagram looks different because we now are looking at one row of sections from the townships to the north, south, east and west of our township.

Section 6 is **contiguous with sections 5, 7 and 8** inside this township and also **sections 12, 1, 36, 31 and 32** from neighboring townships. The answer would be one of the first three – 5, 7 or 8 – and one of the last five – 12, 1, 36, 31 or 32.

Government Lot

A **government lot** refers to any section with irregular borders because of a natural feature such as a mountain, lake or river.

Dividing Sections

In moving to sections, we have taken the state of Arizona, divided it first into 36-square mile townships and then to one square mile sections. But we can go smaller from here by dividing sections.

Sections always are divided by halves and quarters. That's all. And they can be divided multiple times, always by halves and quarters, to identify increasingly smaller parcels of land.

Let's start with one full section ... this section is **one mile** or **5,280 feet** on each side and contains **640 acres**.

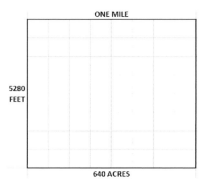

Now we are going to divide that section by quartering it. When you quarter a section, the **linear dimensions** are divided by two and the **area** is divided by four.

Each side of this quarter section is **½ mile** or **2,640 feet** (dividing the mile in half) and the area is **160 acres** (dividing the 640 acres by four.)

Let's quarter this quarter section ...

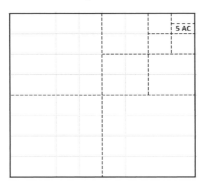

Now we are down to a 40-acre parcel. And if we quarter this again …

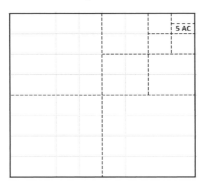

We also can halve a section (or partial section) at any point. For example, we can cut that 10-acre parcel in half to create two 5-acre parcels.

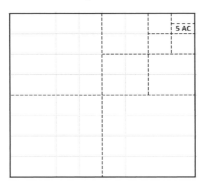

Identifying Parcels

The parcel we created on the previous page would be written as the **S½ NE¼ NE¼ NE¼** of whatever section that is, so let's just say Section 7.

S½ NE¼ NE¼ NE¼ Section 7

When reading a rectangular survey legal description, we always **start at the right** – the largest parcel – **and work our way left**.

The good news is questions about rectangular survey solve themselves. All you need to remember is everything you see is a different instruction. With that in mind, let's try and re-create that parcel. **S½ NE¼ NE¼ NE¼ Section 7.**

Starting at the right, we begin with a full section …

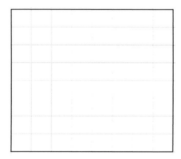

S½ NE¼ NE¼ **NE¼** Section 7 – now we quarter the section and choose the northeast corner.

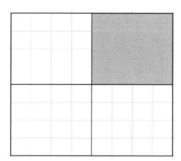

S½ NE¼ **NE¼** NE¼ Section 7 – moving to the left, again we quarter the section and choose the northeast corner.

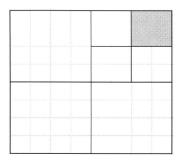

S½ **NE¼** NE¼ NE¼ Section 7 – moving left again, we quarter the section a third time and choose the northeast corner.

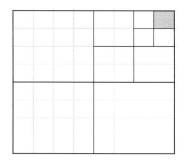

S½ NE¼ NE¼ NE¼ Section 7 – and finally, we halve this last bit into north and south halves. If the description said E or W, we'd divided vertically.

As you can see, we have a match … just by letting the problem solve itself.

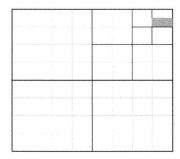

Calculating Acreage

Just as the legal description solves itself when trying to find a parcel, it does the same thing when we're trying to figure out the number of acres in a parcel.

Let's use that same description as before:

S½ NE¼ NE¼ NE¼ Section 7

We know there are 640 acres in a section, so we start with 640. Now, just work your way from right to left, dividing by the bottom number as you go.

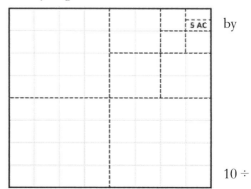

S½ NE¼ NE¼ **NE¼** … first we divided four. 640 ÷ 4 = 160 acres

S½ NE¼ **NE¼** NE¼ … divide by 4 again. 160 ÷ 4 = 40 acres

S½ **NE¼** NE¼ NE¼ … divide by 4 again. 40 ÷ 4 = 10 acres

S½ NE¼ NE¼ NE¼ … now divide by 2. 2 = 5 acres

And again, we have a match with our original diagram.

The only variable to this is if a question contains more than one parcel. If you see either the word **and** or a **semi-colon**, that's a hard stop. Circle the number you have, then start back over at 640 acres before continuing.

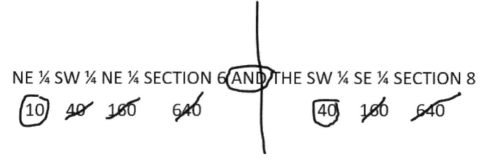

NE ¼ SW ¼ NE ¼ SECTION 6 AND THE SW ¼ SE ¼ SECTION 8

Our answer is **50 acres** … **10** from the first parcel, **40** from the second.

Rectangular Survey with Metes and Bounds

The last acreage problem you might have would combine rectangular survey with a metes and bounds description. Your **point of beginning** would be one corner of a particular parcel, and you find that parcel using rectangular survey.

For example, your point of beginning could be the southwest corner of our shaded parcel – **the southwest corner of the S½ NE¼ NE¼ NE¼ Section 7.**

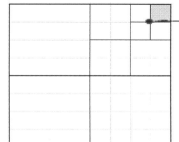

From there, follow the metes and bounds description to create the shape of the parcel.

To find the area, multiple the length of each leg of the parcel to get the square footage. If asked about the acreage, then divide by 640.

If your parcel is a triangle and not a square, take your answer and divide it by 2. **We will have more on acreage and perimeter in Chapter 28, Math.**

Elevations and Caissons

Elevation is a parcel's height above or below a set reference point. This reference point is called a **datum**. Our national datum is mean sea level at New York harbor because, as we all know, New York is the center of the universe!

So, when we talk about Flagstaff sitting at more than 7,000 feet, the city is located more than 7,000 feet above mean sea level at New York Harbor. If you drive to San Diego and see the water storage to the south of Interstate 8 with sea level painted above your head, that's because the land you're driving on is a couple dozen feet below sea level at New York Harbor.

The U.S. Geological Survey has created its own reference points, separate from the national datum, called **benchmarks**. These usually are marked with brass caps showing the elevation.

A **caisson** is the footing for a bridge. The practical application for real estate is if a developer purchases the air rights over a parcel, they also need to own the physical parcels on either side in order to build a structure.

Chapter 12
Land Development and Zoning

As we discussed under government rights, land development and zoning fall under the government's right of police power. A reminder – everything that relates to statute or ordinance is a function of police power.

General Plan

Most municipalities, whether on the county, city or town level, has a general zoning plan. This basically is the city's long-term plan mapping out how the city will grow and what type of properties will be located where. Zoning is the guide for this plan.

Master Planned Communities

Master planned communities are sub-areas of the zoning plans. These master planned communities are more than just the houses contained within. There usually are substantial amenities – walking paths, parks, community centers, perhaps golf courses – as part of the community. It's designed to be one-stop living, where there's no need to leave except to work.

Examples in the Phoenix area including Vistancia, the Dobson Ranch, Verrado and Anthem.

Zoning

Zoning is a municipality's way of controlling the way properties can be used. In addition, zoning can be used to **promote the health and safety** of a community and to **support property values**, which in turn help the area's tax base.

Zoning Terminology
- **Setbacks** – areas on the edges of a property on which nothing can be built. Step outside your garage and you'll see all the houses are on the same line. This is the front setback.
- **Buffer zones** – these are types of zoning separating two others. For example, if there is a gas station on the corner and behind it a supermarket. Behind the

supermarket are apartments and then single-family homes. The apartments can be considered a buffer zone between the retail and the single-family homes beyond.

- **Spot zoning** – changing the zoning for one parcel without changing the master plan.

Non-Conforming/Grandfathered Use

A **non-conforming** or **grandfathered use** is an extending use that does not match the current zoning, but has been grandfathered in. For example, on the southeast corner of 83rd Avenue and Bell there was a little yellow house where In-N-Out Burger now stands. Long after Arrowhead Towne Center and the surrounding shopping centers were zoned commercial and built, this house remained even though the parcel was now zoned commercial. This house still could still be there now if the owners wanted, as a grandfathered use remains as long as the property **is not abandoned, destroyed or expanded in a way that extends the non-conforming use.**

Variances

A **variance** is an exception to the zoning plan that does not change the actual zoning. For example, a fortune teller or insurance agent operating out of a residential house would do so under a variance. In the Phoenix area, there are a number of such properties, particularly in the area once known as Christown near Bethany Home and 19th Avenue.

Natural Area Open Space

In a **Natural Area Open Space (NAOS)**, the land has to be kept in substantially the same condition as it currently exists. In these areas, if construction takes place, you'll see displaced plants labeled so they can be put back in their original location after construction. Much of north and northeast Scottsdale falls under an NAOS designation.

Arizona 811

If you've ever listened to an Arizona Diamondbacks game on the radio, you've heard the ads for the **blue stake hotline**. Property owners are required to call 8-1-1 before digging on their property to give the utility companies a chance to mark the location of underground water, gas and electric lines. Failure to call can leave a property owner liable for any damage to the lines beneath. By the way, these underground utility lines are an excellent example of an **easement in gross**.

Planned Communities/HOAs

A **homeowners association** is a non-profit corporation that manages a particular housing development, be it a subdivision, condominium, townhouse, etc. The **HOA** can levy special assessments for common areas and charge regular HOA dues. The **HOA** enforces its own bylaws and **CC&Rs (covenants, conditions and restrictions.)**

When someone purchases in an HOA, the buyer must receive a copy of the HOA's bylaws and CC&Rs **within 10 days of contract acceptance**. There are other requirements – financial statements, an analysis of the HOA's reserves, information on special assessments and pending litigation – but the bylaws and the CC&Rs are the most important items for our purposes.

KEY IDEAS TO REMEMBER:
- If there are fewer than 50 units, it is the seller's responsibility to provide the HOA information.
- If there are more than 50 units, it is the HOA's responsibility to provide the HOA information.
- An HOA can charge up to $400 for these documents.

Federal Interstate Land Disclosure Act

The **Federal Interstate Land Disclosure Act** is a federal law that deals with the sale of vacant land sight unseen across state lines. The only provision to know for our purposes is that, once a buyer receives a property report, they have a seven-day rescission period.

New Home Sales

We already discussed the need for a developer to produce a public report before selling new homes. It also is important to know that **earnest deposits** are placed in the builders' operating account, not a neutral escrow account as with resale homes. And the builders' reps in the sales office **only represent the builder, never the buyer**.

Chapter 13
Encumbrances

An **encumbrance** is a non-possessory interest in real property that burdens the title to the property. Basically, another party has some sort of interest in a particular piece of real property but neither owns nor possesses it. An **easement**, which we discussed in detail earlier, is an example of an encumbrance – someone has the right of use of a piece of real property without actually owning it. But easements are not the only encumbrances.

Deed Restrictions/CC&Rs

Developers often will include either **deed restrictions** or **covenants, conditions and restrictions (CCR&S)** because they want to control the future nature of their development. While we usually associate CC&Rs with homeowner associations, even properties outside of an HOA usually have CC&Rs attached.

KEY IDEAS TO REMEMBER:
- An HOA cannot prevent or charge homeowners for placing a for sale or for rent sign in their yards. Also, the HOA cannot dictate the type of sign used.
- An HOA cannot prevent installation of solar equipment, though the HOA can dictate how and where the panels need to be placed.

Encroachments

Technically speaking, an **encroachment** is not an encumbrance. But, like an encumbrance, it does place a burden on the title to the property. Encroachments, remember, are inanimate objects that cross the property line – tree branches over a fence, a fence or driveway in the wrong place, etc.

Clouds on Title

Like encroachments, **clouds on title** are not technically encumbrances, but they can create issues for a seller. A cloud on the title is anything that makes the title less than marketable, something that would need to be resolved before title can convey. Examples could be an incorrectly spelled name, an incorrect or incomplete legal address, etc.

Improperly resolved **liens** also can become clouds on the title.

Liens

Liens are the most common encumbrance we see. A lien is a financial encumbrance, a way for a creditor to make sure they're going to get repaid. If a property owner doesn't pay, the creditor can enforce the lien and, in some cases, take ownership of the property through foreclosure.

Classification of Liens

There are a few different ways to classify liens. As with classification of contracts, these are not mutually exclusive categories.

General vs. Specific

A **general lien** attaches to both real and personal property. This would be a judgment or an IRS lien. A **specific lien** attaches to one specific parcel of real property. This would be property taxes, a home loan, special assessments and mechanic's liens.

Voluntary vs. Involuntary

A **voluntary lien** is what it sounds like – a lien that a property owner voluntarily put in place. Your home loan, or a second loan for a pool or solar, would be voluntary liens. An **involuntary lien** is a lien where the property owner had no say in the matter. Property taxes, special assessments and judgments would be involuntary liens.

Equitable vs. Statutory

A **statutory lien** has a basis in statute. Property tax liens, for example, are statutory liens because there is a specific law that says property taxes create a lien. **Equitable liens** are not based on statute. Home loans, for instance, are equitable liens – we agree to the lien, but they are not required by law.

Liens (other than mechanics liens) take priority as of the date and time recorded within their category. So, no matter when a lien for a home loan is filed, it never can have higher priority than property taxes or special assessments.

Mechanics Liens

Mechanics liens are liens used by a contractor when they perform work but the homeowner does not pay for the work done. Keep in mind, the person filing the lien doesn't have to be a contractor, but it's easier to use the term for our purposes.

Mechanics liens only can be filed either for improvements made to the property or the materials for those improvements. So, a lumber supplier or contractor can file a mechanic lien. A cleaning company, which is not improving the property, could not.

Because mechanics liens only are the start of the process and the contractor still needs to secure a judgment in court, these leans are considered **inchoate**. Inchoate means incomplete.

KEY IDEAS TO REMEMBER:
- Contractors must provide the property owner with a pre-lien notice within 20 days after the start of work. Without this notice, no lien can be filed later.
- Contractors must file the mechanics lien within 120 days of the completion of work.
- Contractors then have six months to secure a judgment against the property owner.
- On residential properties, only the GENERAL contractor – the contractor who has a signed contract with the owner – can file a mechanics lien.
- On commercial properties, both GENERAL and SUBCONTRACTORS can file. A subcontractor even can file a mechanics lien against the property if the property owner paid the general, but the general didn't pay the subs.
- On commercial properties, mechanics liens only can be filed against the tenant spaces – not the building as a whole – and the tenant improvements.

Unlike most liens, which take priority as of the date and time recorded, mechanics liens take effect as of the date the work started.

For example, let's say a homeowner has a pool installed beginning July 1 and ending October. The same homeowner has their bathroom remodeled starting August 1 and ending August 31. And this same homeowner doesn't pay either contractor, so both file mechanics liens. The lien for the pool has a higher priority because work started on July 1.

Doctrine of Laches

Laches is whenever someone has lost their legal right to sue because of an undue delay. If a contractor doesn't file the mechanics lien within 120 days of the completion of work or doesn't get the judgment within the six months, laches applies and the contractor's out of luck.

Judgments

A **judgment** – a court ruling that one party owns another financial compensation – also creates a lien. These are general liens, attaching to both real and personal property. Judgments have to be recorded at the county recorder's office to be valid.

Lis Pendens, Judgments and Writs of Execution

- **Lis pendens** is notice of legal action pending regarding a piece of property. Basically, this means that a lawsuit has been filed.
- A **judgment** is issued when the lawsuit has been won.
- A **writ of execution** then is issued, authorizing an officer of the court to seize and sell as much property needed to satisfy the judgment.

KEY IDEA TO REMEMBER:

- First you file (lis pendens), then you win (judgment), then you collect (writ of execution).

IRS Liens

The IRS doesn't like being ignored. If you don't pay the IRS, they can place a lien on your property enforceable on both real and personal property. If you still don't pay your income taxes, the IRS can enforce a tax **levy**, where the IRS will seize whatever assets are necessary in lieu of payment.

Chapter 14
Acquisition and Transfer of Title

It's important to understand not just the different ways that ownership – title to property – can transfer but also the different types of deeds used as well as the basics of title insurance.

KEY IDEA TO REMEMBER:

- A deed is the piece of paper used to convey or grant ownership. Title is more of the concept of ownership. If someone owns a property, we say they have title to that property.

Thinking back to our ORs and EEs, when title to property conveys, we say that the deed is granted from the grantor to the grantee.

Methods of Transfer

The technical term for transferring title is **alienation**. Think of it as the grantor is being alienated from their property. Alienation can be either voluntary or involuntary.

Voluntary Alienation

Voluntary alienation can take place through a sale, dedication, gift or will.

- **Sale –** just as it sounds, the seller voluntarily sells their property to a buyer
- **Dedication –** a private individual gives property to the government. In many towns, for example, owners of one of the original homesites donate the house to the town for a museum.
- **Gift –** property is transferred between individuals without monetary consideration.

Will

The person who creates the will is called a **testator** and the will is known as a **testament**. When someone dies with a will in place, they are said to have died **testate**. While their dying likely wasn't voluntary, the **testator** (now known as the **decedent** after their death) did decide how they wanted their property distributed. If someone dies without a will, the term is **intestate**.

The vast majority of wills have to go through **probate**. Probate is a court proceeding to determine if there is a valid will and to distribute the debts and assets of the **decedent**.

If someone is named in the will to distribute the estate, they are considered the **executor**. If someone dies interstate, an **administrator** will be assigned to distribute the estate.

KEY IDEAS TO REMEMBER:
- Paired terms to know – will/testate/executor; intestate /administrator

Involuntary Alienation

When someone dies intestate, this is an example of **involuntary alienation** since the decedent did not proactively choose how the estate will be distributed. Other examples of involuntary alienation include the government rights of eminent domain and escheat, and enforcement of liens (foreclosure). Another version of involuntary alienation is **adverse possession**.

Adverse Possession

As we discussed with prescriptive easements, there are four requirements to gain a property through adverse possession. The use of the property has to be **open, notorious, hostile** and **continuous.**

- Open – that the use is not being hidden.
- Notorious – that anyone paying attention would observe the property in use.
- Hostile – that the use is without the owner's permission.
- Continuous – that the use has occurred for at least 10 years.

KEY IDEAS TO REMEMBER:
- Tacking – the ability to tack on one's use onto prior use to create a full 10-year period – applies to adverse possession as well.
- To gain ownership, the party using the property would go to court and file a prescriptive suit.
- License – permission to use the property – ends the possibility of adverse possession because the use no longer is hostile.
- Adverse possession cannot take place on government-owned property.

Note: While it's easiest to think of adverse possession in terms of someone living in an abandoned house, don't confuse adverse possession with "squatting." In Arizona, we don't have squatter's rights in the same manner as many other states do. Generally speaking, people cannot create a legal right to occupy a property without going through the full adverse possession requirements.

Conveyance Deeds

While there are several types of deeds about which you can be asked, there only are three deeds primarily uses to convey ownership – **general warranty**, **special warranty** and **bargain and sale**. The difference between the three deeds are the promises the grantor makes to grantee regarding the quality of the title.

Covenants and Warranties

With any deed, there are five possible covenants and warranties:

a) **Covenant of seizin** – the grantor promises they own the property and have the right to convey ownership of it.

b) **Covenant of quiet enjoyment** – the grantor promises that the grantee will be able to enjoy ownership of their property without being disturbed by any claims on their title.

c) **Covenant against further encumbrances** – the grantor promises the grantee that there are no encumbrances that have not been disclosed.

d) **Warranty of further assurance** – the grantor promises the grantee that they will correct or perfect the title as necessary during their lifetime.

e) **Warranty of warranty forever** – the grantor promises the grantee that they always will defend the grantee against any legal claims on their title.

KEY IDEAS TO REMEMBER:
- Marketable title does not need to be free and clear of all encumbrances, only undisclosed encumbrances. For example, a buyer generally accepts that a property tax lien will survive the close of escrow.
- The covenant of quiet enjoyment is a buyer's best claim to ownership, since the seller has said there will be no one making claims of ownership.

General Warranty Deed

A **general warranty deed**, also known simply as a **warranty** deed, comes with all the covenants and warranties. The buyer receives A, B, C, D and E from the list above. This is the most common deed used and provides both the **most liability for the grantor** and **most protection for the grantee**.

Special Warranty Deed

A **special warranty deed**, also known as a **limited warranty** deed, comes with the three covenants and the warranty of further assurance. These typically are used on corporate relocations and bank-owned homes. The buyer receives A, B, C and D **but not** E.

Bargain and Sale Deed

A **bargain and sale deed** comes with the three covenants and no (sometimes worded as implied) warranties. The buyer receives A, B and C and that's it. A sheriff's or trustee's deed at the end of judicial or non-judicial foreclosure; a treasurers deed at the end of a tax lien sale or an executor's deed through probate all would be bargain and sale deeds. The bargain and sale deed provides the **least liability for the grantor** and the **least protection for the grantee**.

Special Purpose Deeds

Quit Claim Deed

A **quit claim** deed typically is used either to clear a cloud on the title or to convey the grantor's interest in a property without any covenants or warranties. The grantee receives whatever interest the grantor has. For example, a couple gets divorced and the wife is receiving the house. The husband would sign a quit claim deed to convey his interest to her with no covenants or warranties attached.

KEY IDEA TO REMEMBER:
- Quit claim deeds are used after ownership and convey whatever interest the grantor has.

Disclaimer Deed

A **disclaimer deed** allows one spouse to purchase real property in severalty – sole and separate from their spouse. Since Arizona is a community property state, when one spouse purchase, the property belongs to both automatically. A disclaimer deed prevents this, leaving the property only in the name of the one spouse who purchased.

KEY IDEA TO REMEMBER:
- Disclaimer deeds are used before ownership.

Patent Deed

A **patent deed** is the original title to a property given by a government entity to a private individual.

Requirements for a Valid Deed

For a deed to be valid, it needs to:

- Have legally competent parties – each over 18 or emancipated and of sound mind.
  - o Duress or menace could allow a person to claim to be temporarily mentally incompetent
- Be in writing, per the statute of frauds.
- Have a valid legal description – metes and bounds, lot and block or rectangular survey.
- Have a definite grantee – title can't be conveyed to "John and Jane Doe" unless the new owners really are named John and Jane Doe.
- Valid consideration – either valuable (money, goods or services) or good (love and affection).

Title officially conveys when there has been **delivery and acceptance** of the deed. In Arizona, deeds **do not have to be recorded to be valid**. Responsibility to record the deed is on the grantee and, while not required, it's not a particularly brilliant idea not to record the deed.

Delivery and acceptance either can be from grantor directly to grantee or from grantor to a third party (think escrow company) with instructions to give the deed to the grantee. Once it has been accepted by the grantee, ownership officially has conveyed.

Recording the deed provides **constructive notice**. This is public notice, meaning once recorded in the county recorder's office for the county in which the property is located, any member of the public can search the county records and find the record.

Constructive notice is different than **actual notice**, which is what one person sees or hears.

For example, if you see a moving truck in your neighbor's driveway, you have actual notice that they are moving. When you check the county records and see they no longer are on the deed, you now have constructive notice that they sold. (And if you're licensed, you are entitled to be angry with them for not listing their home with you!)

Affidavit of Value

When a deed is recorded in Arizona, it must be accompanied by an **affidavit of value**. The affidavit of value is a notarized statement signed by buyer and seller and listing the sales price. The county assessor will use the information on the affidavit of value to help determine tax values for the following year.

Title Insurance

When a grantor conveys title to property to a grantee, the grantor is expected to provide **marketable title** – title free of any undisclosed encumbrances. Of the three methods used to provide evidence of marketable title – an abstract and attorney's opinion, the Torrens system and title insurance – only title insurance is used in Arizona.

Title insurance is the free-market solution for providing marketable title. As long as a title insurance company is willing to put up their money if title isn't marketable, that's good enough for us.

Evidence of marketable title comes through the **preliminary title report** and eventual **title** commitment that comes at the end of escrow.

The title report contains three sections:

- Boilerplate – the basic wording and limits applicable to all policies
- **Schedule A** – all the details of the current transaction:
  - o Name of buyer and seller
  - o Sales price
  - o Name of lender, if there is one
  - o Loan amount
- **Schedule B** – all the exceptions to the policy. In other words, all disclosed encumbrances on the title, which may include:
  - o Easements
  - o Property tax liens
  - o Mortgage/deed of trust liens
  - o Income tax liens or judgments against the seller
  - o CC&Rs

Types of policies

There are two types of title insurance policies – a **standard** policy and an **extended** policy – with the difference between the two being the coverage offered. Both policies are paid with a one-time premium charged at close of escrow. The **seller** buys the **buyer** and **owners policy**. The **buyer** buys an **extended** policy for the **lender**. The extended policy also may be known as the lender's, mortgagee's, broadform or ALTA policy.

KEY IDEA TO REMEMBER:

- Zoning is not addressed anywhere in the title insurance commitment and zoning changes never are covered because there is no compensation because of rezoning.

A standard policy will cover **forgery** or **title company errors** but will not cover anything that the buyer should have resolved during their due diligence period – **survey errors, adverse possession, unrecorded mechanics liens** and **disclosed gaps in the chain of title**. The extended policy **covers everything above**.

Subrogation

Subrogation is substituting one creditor for another. In the context of title insurance, if a title insurance company has to pay a claim because of someone else's mistake, the title insurer will go after whoever made the error in an effort to be made whole. That's subrogation.

Chapter 15
Escrow and Settlement

Escrow is the process of compiling all the paperwork and handling all of the funds to make sure a transaction goes smoothly. **Escrow companies** handle both the paperwork and the money for the transaction, following instructions provided in the **purchase contract**.

Escrow companies do not write contracts and cannot read intent into what is in the contract. The responsibility for a properly prepared contract falls on the **licensee** and, by extension, **their broker**. The **broker** ultimately is responsible for all the activities involved in escrow.

Real estate agents and brokers are not parties to the purchase contract and therefore are not parties to an escrow. **Buyers** and **sellers**, obviously, are the primary parties involved in an escrow.

Settlement statements

The **closing disclosure** is the main settlement statement used in a real estate transaction when a loan is involved. On cash transactions, a streamlined settlement statement is used. In either case, the purpose of the settlement statement is to disclose and reconcile the debits and credits involved in a closing to show what the buyer needs to bring in to close and what the seller's proceeds will be.

KEY IDEAS TO REMEMBER:
- A debit is funds owed to close a transaction.
- A credit is funds received as part of a closing.

If a seller has more debits than credits, the seller has to **write a check to close escrow**.

Debits and credits are one area where I urge students to take a step back and think about how the money is flowing. Is a given item something that involves the buyer, the seller or both? And is this money that one party owes in general, will receive in general or is paying to the other side.

Memorization of every possible item on a settlement statement is overwhelming to the point of being almost impossible. It's far better to visualize ...

How the Money Flows

- Buyer Debits
  - Purchase price ←——————→
  - Closing costs
  - Taxes/Prorations in Advance ←——→
  - Hazard Insurance
  - Impounds (2 mos)
  - Pre-paid mtg interest

- Seller Credits
  - Purchase price
  - Taxes/Prorations in Advance

- Buyer Credits
  - New loan
  - Loan assumption ←——————→
  - Taxes/prorations in Arrears ←——→
  - Earnest deposit/add'l down
  - Seller concessions ←——————→
  - Security deposits ←——————→
  - Rents ←——————————→

- Seller Debits
  - Payoff existing loan
  - Loan assumption
  - Taxes/prorations in Arrears
  - Closing Costs/Commissions
  - Seller concessions
  - Security deposits
  - Rents

The largest debit a buyer has – the largest amount of money they need to bring in to close – is the purchase price. At the same time, that purchase price is the largest credit the seller receives. That's the pile of cash they agreed to.

Buyers also have to bring in funds to cover closing costs, taxes or prorations the seller paid in advance, their hazard insurance, impound accounts and pre-paid mortgage interest. **(We will discuss these ideas more in Chapter 28, Math).**

The only other credit a seller really receives is cash from the buyer for anything the seller paid in advance.

Buyers receive a number of credits. The largest is their new loan. **The loan is a debt, not a debit**. It's really a large pile of cash the lender is giving the buyer to offset some of the purchase price. If the buyer is assuming the seller's loan, it's a credit to the buyer – money they don't have to bring in – and a debit to the seller, because they're accepting loan forgiveness rather than cash.

On rental properties, both security deposits and rents are credits to the buyer and debits to the seller. We know security deposits belong to the tenants, so the seller has to give that tenant money to the buyer so the buyer has it when a tenant moves out. Rents are paid in advance for the month by the tenant. If the seller sells mid-month, the seller didn't earn that full rent. The buyer receives a prorated portion for the time that the buyer is the new landlord.

Like I said, the best way to approach credit and debit questions is to take a step back and think about how the money is moving. Short of that, if you feel compelled to try and memorize something, use the chart above.

Disbursing Commissions

As we've discussed, commissions belong to the **employing broker** and the employing broker then pays the commission to the sales associate. The employing broker can give the escrow company instructions to pay the sales associate directly, either through a check or wired funds, rather than having one large check sent to the employing broker for further processing. Escrow officers always will ask agents and brokerages to provide commission instructions, signed by the designated broker.

Double Escrows/Simultaneous Closings

For our purposes, a **double escrow** happens when an investor is purchasing a property and immediately selling that property to a new buyer. The key idea here is **disclosure**. The investor has to disclose to the eventual buyer that they are selling a property they do not yet own.

This commonly is called a simultaneous closing because the investor is closing on their purchase and then simultaneously (or close enough) closing on their sale.

Tax requirements

Escrow offers, as part of the title search, will verify whether the seller has any **tax liens** or **tax levies** that need to be cleared as part of the closing. A **tax lien** is a lien placed by the IRS against a property because the owner hasn't paid their taxes. A **tax levy** happens when the IRS seizes the taxpayer's property in lieu of payments not made.

FIRPTA

The escrow officer also has to make sure the **Foreign Investment Real Property Tax Act (FIRPTA)** is applied when a foreign national is selling real property. FIRPTA requires **buyers** to withhold a portion of the sales price from a foreign national selling property, setting the money aside for the IRS to cover capital gains that normally would be paid. In reality, the escrow company handles the set aside.

Chapter 16
Fair Housing and the ADA

Fair housing can be simplified down to two concepts. First, treat everyone with respect. Second, don't be a bigoted, racist, xenophobic jerk. From a testing standpoint, however, there only are a handful of items that you will need to know.

Fair Housing Laws

The "Slavery" Amendments
- The **13th Amendment** abolished slavery
- The **14th Amendment** granted citizenship to the slaves and included due process clauses
- The **15th Amendment** provided voting rights to all male citizens

Of the three, the 13th Amendment is the most likely to be tested.

Civil Rights Act of 1866
The **Civil Rights Act of 1866** prohibited discrimination based on **race** in all real property transactions.

Plessy v. Ferguson/Brown v. Board of Education
- Plessy v. Ferguson established the concept of separate but equal public accommodations
- Brown v. Board of Education abolished the same concept of separate but equal facilities

Fair Housing Act (Title VIII of the 1968 Civil Rights Act)
The **Fair Housing Act** prohibited discrimination in the sale, rental or advertisement of real property transactions and real estate brokerage services based on four protected

classes – **race**, **color**, **religion** and **national origin**. Subsequent amendments added **sex/gender**, **familiar status** and **disability** as additional protected classes.

Summarizing the protected classes:

- 1866 – Race only
- 1968 – Race, color, national origin and religion
- 1974 – Added sex/gender
- 1988 – Added familial status/disability

Note: Make sure you know the years on the above bullet points as they are testable.

Definitions

- **Familial Status** – the short definition is any household with a child under 18. Pregnant woman and those in the process of obtaining custody to a child under 18 also are protected here
- **Disability** – any physical or mental impairment that impacts one or more major life activity

Familial Status and Multifamily Real Estate

- Landlords can't charge either "kid rent" or "kid deposits." Kids are not pets!
- Landlords cannot have separate family areas or family facilities, such as pool. Everyone must be able to use all facilities and live in any available unit.

Disability Impacts on Real Estate

- Landlords must make **reasonable accommodations** in their rules for disabled tenants. For instance, pet deposits and no pet policies do not apply to service animals.
- Landlords must allow a tenant to make **reasonable modifications** to a unit so that they can use it as fully as a non-disabled tenant. Think grab bars, ramps, wider doorways, etc. The tenant is responsible for the cost of these modifications. In addition, the landlord can require the tenant to put the property back in substantially the same condition at the end of the lease.
- **All common areas must be accessible**.
- Landlords **cannot charge** disabled tenants **extra** for parking.
- In multi-story buildings without an elevator, only the ground floor need be accessible.

- At new build communities, only the **sales office** must be accessible, **not the models**.

The Three Big No Nos

- **Steering** – guiding clients towards or away from any given area based on their membership in a protected class. You also can see this described as taking clients where you believe that they would be most comfortable based on your own opinion.
- **Blockbusting** – "knock knock … did you see who moved in down the block? You've got to sell now before values drop." In short, encouraging sellers to sell because of the presence of a member of a protected class.
- **Redlining** – this is where a lender literally would draw a red line on a map and refuse to make any loans in the area without regard to financial qualifications.

Enforcement

The **Fair Housing Enforcement Office** (part of the **Department of Housing and Urban Development – HUD)** enforces the Fair Housing Act. In Arizona, Fair Housing complaints also can be filed with the **Arizona Attorney General** because our laws have been ruled stricter than the federal laws.

KEY IDEAS TO REMEMBER:

- Fair Housing complaints must be filed within one year of the alleged discrimination
- HUD must start the investigation within 30 days and complete it within 100 days

Fines for Fair Housing Violations

- 1st offense – up to $16,000
- 2nd offense – up to $37,500
- 3rd offense – up to $65,000

Needless to say, violating Fair Housing laws also will likely cost the violator their real estate license.

Exceptions

While there are four primary exceptions to the Fair Housing act, for our purposes we only need to be worried about two. Make sure you know that there are **no exceptions based on race. Ever. Period.**

For Sale by Owner

If someone owns **three or fewer properties**, does not use any **discriminating advertising** or the **services of a real estate brokerage**, they can discriminate to their heart's content against any protected class other than race.

Rooms for Rent – Mrs. Murphy's Boarding House Rule

With **rooms for rent**, if the property consists of **four or fewer units** and the **owner occupies one of the units**, they can discriminate to their heart's content against any protected class other than race as long as they **don't use discriminatory advertising** or the **services of a real estate brokerage.**

Equal Credit Opportunity Act

The **Equal Credit Opportunity Act** prohibits discriminatory lending practices. For our purposes, the ECOA adds three protected classes to the seven already in place through Fair Housing – **age**, **marital status** and **dependence on public assistance**.

KEY IDEA TO REMEMBER:
- Yes, marital status takes the place of familial status in the ECOA. Having said that, it's much easier to just add the three protected classes to the existing seven of race, color, national origin, religion, gender/sex, familial status and disability.

Advertising Requirements

Real estate licensees must include a **fair housing logo** or **slogan** in all of their advertising, from business cards to websites to flyers and for sale signs. In addition, all real estate brokers must have a **fair housing posted** visible in a prominent location to indicate they comply with Fair Housing laws.

Licensees must be careful in the images and words they use in their advertising so as to not convey a preference of one group of buyers over another.

For example: if I listed a house across the street from the Mormon Temple in Mesa, I never would reference the temple as that indicates a preference for one particular religious group. I would reference the Temple District, however, as that is a geographic area designated by the city of Mesa.

Americans with Disabilities Act (ADA)

The **Americans with Disabilities Act** was passed in 1990 and provides extensive protections from discrimination for those with disabilities. Again, a disability is defined as a **physical or mental impairment that impacts one or more life activities.**

There are five sections under the ADA but, for our purposes, there only are two you need to know:

- **Title 1** – Deals with the hiring and managing of employees. Requires employers with 15 or more employees to provide reasonable accommodations for disabled employees as long as it doesn't create an undue burden on the business.
- **Title 3** – Deals with public buildings. In short, someone with a disability needs to be able to go wherever the public can go. For building entrances, if there are stairs, there needs to be a ramp.

Fines for violating the ADA are **$75,000 for the first offense, $150,000 for the second offense**.

Additional Items to Know

Jones v. Mayer

Jones v. Mayer was a 1968 Supreme Court case dealing with discriminatory deed restrictions.

KEY IDEAS TO REMEMBER:
- The Supreme Court ruled that discriminatory deed restrictions are unenforceable. They don't have to be removed, but they can't be enforced.
- The decision affirmed the Civil Rights Act of 1968.

Age Restricted Developments

There are exceptions in the Fair Housing Act for what euphemistically is called "housing for older persons." These simply are the active adult or retirement communities we all know. In short, an age restricted development **does not have to follow Fair Housing restrictions regarding familial status** and **can restrict children from living in the community.**

There are two types of age-restricted developments:

- **62 and up** – all residents must be 62 or older. Period.
- **55 and up** – in a 55+ community, at least 80 percent of the units must have at least one resident who is 55 and older.

Group Homes

Municipalities and HOAs need to be careful about how they handle group homes as, depending on the mission of the group home, restricting their presence could violate Fair Housing laws.

Chapter 17
Leases and Leasehold Estates

As we discussed in Chapter 5, estates can be either freehold – ownership and possession – or leasehold – possession only. Again, a leasehold estate is exactly what it sounds like. Someone is leasing a property from someone else.

KEY IDEAS TO REMEMBER:

- **The lessor or landlord creates a leasehold estate for the lessee or tenant.**
- **The lease is considered to be chattel real – personal property, or chattel, relating to real estate.**

NOTE: If you see any reference to chattel real, it **always** refers to a lease.

Types of Leasehold Estates

There are four types of leasehold estates, two based on elements of time and two passed on the positions of the lessor and lessee.

Estate for Years

An **estate for years** is a leasehold estate with a **set starting and ending date**. It doesn't matter if the lease is for years, months, weeks or day. If there is a set starting and ending date, this is an estate for years.

Estate from Period to Period

An **estate from period to period**, sometimes referred to as **periodic tenancy**, is a leasehold estate where there is a set time frame with no specific end date. Year-to-year, month-to-month, week-to-week and day-to-day leases all would create estates from period to period.

KEY IDEAS TO REMEMBER:

- A lease for January, February and March is an estate for years because the leasehold begins January 1 and ends March 31.
- A month-to-month lease beginning January 1 is an estate from period to period because there is no specified ending date.

- A 30-day notice is required to terminate a month-to-month lease. A 10-day notices is required to terminate a week-to-week lease.

Estate at Will

An **estate at will** exists when a lessor or landlord allows a lessee or tenant to remain on the property indefinitely, either after completion of a lease or in general. We say this is an estate at will because the tenant is on the property with the permission of, or at the will of, the landlord.

Estate at Sufferance

An **estate at sufferance** exists when a tenant refuses to leave a property after the lease has expired. The tenant now has become a **holdover tenant**. We say this is an estate at sufferance because the landlord is suffering from their inability to regain possession to their property.

Elements of a Valid Lease

For a lease to be valid it must include a property address, consideration to be given by the lessee and terms of possession. It also must be **signed by the lessor**. The lessee **does not** have to sign the lease for it to be valid because they are not surrendering any legal rights, unlike the landlord, who is surrendering possession.

Types of Leases

There are several types of leases you may be asked about:

- **Graduated lease** – lease payments start low and increase over time. Think of this is an introductory rate paired with the actual rent later.
- **Percentage lease** – used almost exclusively in retail, the landlord receives a portion of the business' sales. The tenants in Arrowhead Towne Center, for example, have percentage leases and pay a percentage of their annual sales to the landlord.
- **Net lease** – again used in commercial, the tenant pays a flat amount of rent and a prorated percentage of the building's taxes, insurance and maintenance.
- **Gross lease** – this is the norm in residential, where the tenant pays a flat amount of rent and the landlord is responsible for taxes, property taxes, etc.
- **Ground lease** – more common to commercial, one party leases the ground beneath whatever buildings and improvements are added. The Pavilions in

Scottsdale, for example, are on a ground lease – one party owns the shopping center, but is leasing the land on a long-term basis from the Salt River Pima Maricopa Indian Community.

- **Sale and leaseback** – a developer constructs a building, sells it, then leases it back on a long-term lease. Builders often to this with their model homes.

Assignment, Subleasing and Other Concepts

A **sublease** takes place when a tenant or lessee turns around and leases the property to another person. The original lessee becomes the **sublessor** and the new tenant is the **sublessee**.

An **assignment** takes place when a tenant assigns their leasehold interest entirely to another party.

KEY IDEAS TO REMEMBER:
- With a sublease, the original lessee is legally responsible for fulfillment of the original lease.
- With a lease assignment, the original lessee is relieved of any further legal responsibility.
- Both generally require landlord or lessor permission.

Contract and Economic Rent

There are two sides to the leasehold coin. What benefits one party usually does so to the detriment of the other. This is key to remember when discussing contract and economic rent, excess or deficit rent and positive or negative leaseholds.

Contract rent is the amount of rent the tenant and landlord agrees upon, as expressed in the lease contract. **Economic** or **market rent** is the theoretical number that a property should rent for. It's the going rent for the area.

When the tenant is paying less than the going rent in the area, in other words **when the contract rent is less than the economic rent**, the tenant is holding a **positive leasehold** because they are paying less than they probably should. At the same time, since the landlord is receiving less than the market says they should, they are receiving **deficit rent**.

On the other hand, when the tenant is paying more than the going rent in an area, in other words **when the contract rent is more than the economic rent**, the tenant is holding a **negative leasehold** because they are paying more than they probably should.

At the same time, since the landlord is receiving more than the market says they should, they are receiving **excess rent**.

Terminating a Lease

Obviously, the most common way that a lease terminates is expiration. When the lease is up, it's up and it's time to go. But there are other one-off scenarios that also can result in lease termination. These include **destruction of the property**, **eminent domain**, **foreclosure** and **surrender and acceptance**.

KEY IDEA TO REMEMBER:

- If a tenant is renting a residential property that has been foreclosed on, their lease remains in effect. The only exception is if the buyer wants the property as an owner-occupied home, they have to provide the tenant with 90 days' notice before they can force the tenant out.

Eviction

We will discuss eviction more when we discuss the Arizona Residential Landlord Tenant Act. For now, just remember there are two types of eviction, **actual** and **constructive**.

KEY IDEAS TO REMEMBER:

- Actual eviction takes place when the tenant is in breach.
- Constructive eviction takes place when the landlord is in breach.

Eviction is involuntary while surrender and acceptance, where the tenant surrenders the property before the lease has expired and the landlord accepts possession back, is a voluntary process.

Other Residential Lease Concepts

Section 8

"Section 8" is a common name for the Housing Choice Voucher Program, funded by the U.S. Department of Housing and Urban Development. The Section 8 program allows private landlords to rent apartments and homes qualified low income tenants, while also receiving a government-subsidized payment.

Short-term and Vacation Rentals

A **short-term** or **vacation rental** is defined as any lease for fewer than 31 days. While municipalities cannot restrict homeowners from turning their properties into short-term or vacation rentals, HOAs absolutely can do so.

Commercial Leasing

Commercial leasing is an entirely different animal than residential and, like almost everything else in the commercial real estate world, has a language all its own.

Tenant Improvements

Commercial tenants often will receive a **tenant improvement allowance** from the landlord. This is money the tenant can use to renovate the interior of their leased space – the **building** shell - to fit their business' needs. Any improvements that cost more than the allowance are the responsibility of the tenant.

Common Area Maintenance Expense

Common area maintenance (CAM) expenses are, just as they sound, expenses for a commercial development's common areas. All the tenants pay a portion of these expenses, prorated based on their comparative square footage.

Expense Stops

Often, a commercial landlord will cover the cost of some common expenses up to a certain amount, even on a net lease, up to a certain level – the **expense stop**. For instance, a landlord can say they will pay a certain amount of the insurance or property taxes for the property. If the insurance or property tax totals rise, the lessees would then cover the expense on a prorated basis.

Turnkey

A **turnkey** property is what it sounds like – a property where the commercial lessee can simply "turn the key" and be ready to go. Think of a pizza place replacing another pizza place. The basics for the business already are in place, so the new lessee can just turn the key, change out the menus and be off and running.

Anchor Tenant

The **anchor tenant** is the largest tenant in a commercial development, the tenant whose presence attracts the most customers, leading to spillover business for everyone else. This could be a supermarket, big box store, gym, etc.

Chapter 18
Arizona Residential Landlord and Tenant Act

Like most states, Arizona has a law designed to protect tenants and establish the bare basics of the landlord-tenant relationship. Ours is called the **Arizona Residential Landlord and Tenant Act**.

While in practice, the law is designed to protect tenants from unscrupulous landlords, make sure you know that the law **clarifies and regulates the relationship between landlords and tenants** because it contains requirements on both parties.

General Provisions

The Arizona Residential Landlord and Tenant Act echoes Fair Housing laws and **prohibits discrimination against tenants with children**, albeit with the same Fair Housing exceptions for age-restricted communities.

There's another provision that allows a tenant who has been the victim of domestic violence to terminate their lease. Once the tenant provides the landlord with written documentation such as a police report or restraining order, the **landlord must release the tenant from the lease within 30 days**.

Bedbugs

Landlords of multi-family properties must provide tenants with **bedbug informational material** and cannot rent any unit which is in the midst of an active bedbug infestation.

Landlord Obligations

Rules

A landlord must provide a tenant with a copy of the unit's rules **at lease signing**. The landlord can change these rules, but must **provide 30 days' notice** before enforcing the changes.

The landlord must provide the tenant with a copy of the lease and tell the tenant in writing that they are entitled to be present at the move-out inspection. Landlords also will provide tenants with a move-in inspection form, detailing any existing damage.

Tenants must be provided contact information for either the landlord or the property manager who is managing the property.

Landlords must tell tenants where they can find a copy of the Arizona Residential Landlord and Tenant Act – the Arizona Department of Housing website.

Finally, the landlord is required to keep the premises in a **fit and habitable** condition.

Security Deposits

Security deposits belong to **the tenant**. The landlord is required to keep this money separate and available for the tenant when the lease is over. The **maximum security deposit a landlord can request is one and one-half times the monthly rent**. The tenant can offer a larger security deposit, but the landlord cannot require it.

The landlord must return the security deposit within **14 business days** of the tenant demanding the money (usually occurring at lease termination.) The landlord **can make reasonable deductions for damage** and has to provide the tenant with an itemized accounting of the deductions.

KEY IDEA TO REMEMBER:
- If the landlord does not return the security deposit less deductions within the 14 business days, the landlord now will be liable for twice the amount wrongfully withheld.

This is NOT the same as three times the security deposit. The security deposit already belongs to the tenant. The penalty out of the landlord's pocket is twice that amount.

The landlord can charge **non-refundable fees** such as pet or cleaning fees, but must disclose the specific purpose of each fee.

Tenant Obligations

The tenant is required to **maintain the property in a fit and habitable condition**, following not just the unit's rules but city health and safety codes.

The tenant must **provide the landlord access** to the property if the landlord has given **48 hours' notice**. The landlord can **enter the property without notice** in the case of an **emergency** or when it's **impracticable** for notice to be provided.

Payment of Rent

Lastly, and most obviously, the tenant must pay their rent. If not specified in the lease, **rent is due on the first of the month** and **is late on the second of the month.**

When a tenant is late with their rent, the first notice given by the landlord is a **five-day notice to quit**. This would be either delivered by hand or certified mail. The tenant has five days to pay the rent, else the landlord then can go to court and file a **forcible detainer**, ordering the tenant to move. If the tenant still doesn't pay, the landlord would seek a **writ of execution**, at which point the sheriff will forcibly remove the tenant from the property.

If the tenant is evicted for failure to pay or any other breach of the lease, the landlord is entitled to keep the security deposit.

Remedies

When either the landlord or the tenant is in non-compliance of the lease regarding an issue of **health or safety, 5 days' notice** to correct is required. For instance, if the air condition stops working or the tenant refuses to treat a bedbug problem, five-day notice to correct the situation would be given. After those five days, the lease can be terminated.

For any other issues not involving either health or safety, or non-payment of rent, **10 days' notice is required**. For instance, a broken garbage disposal is inconvenient, but is not a health and safety issue.

Self-Help for Minor Defects

Rather than terminate their lease when the landlord has not addressed a non-health and safety issue, a tenant is allowed to get the repair done themselves through the **self-help for minor defects** clause. The tenant can have repairs performed, ideally by a licensed contractor and deduct from their rent **the greater of either $300 or one-half month's rent**. The tenant would need to provide receipts for the repairs as well.

Abandonment

When a tenant abandons a property, the property owner can regain possession ahead of the actual lease termination. The landlord must post a **notice of abandonment** for five days before claiming the property was abandoned.

Tenants' Personal Property

The landlord must hold onto to a tenant's personal property **for 14 days** after either abandonment eviction for failure to pay rent. The landlord only can charge the tenant the **reasonable cost of moving and storage** for the tenant to regain their property.

If the tenant does not claim their property, the landlord then can sell the property, apply the proceeds to whatever amount is owed, and then send the balance to the tenant at their last known address.

Distraint

When a landlord seizes a tenant's personal property in lieu of rent paid, this is known as **distraint**. In Arizona, **distraint is illegal on residential properties**. However, it is legal on commercial properties.

Chapter 19
Property Management

Property management statutes are in an entirely different portion of the Arizona Revised Statutes than the Arizona Residential Landlord and Tenant Act. While the landlord-tenant act **clarifies and regulates the relationship between landlord and tenant**, property management regulations define the relationship between property manager and owner.

Licensing

A **real estate license is required** to perform property management services **unless:**

- The property manager is working **at only one property** on a given workday
- AND the property manager **is not being compensated** specifically based on their property management duties. This would apply, for example, to apartment rental agents who receive incentives for each lease they secure

A property owner **absolutely can manage their own property** without a license.

Property Management Agreements

A **property management agreement** must include the names of both the **property owner** and **property manager** and **must be signed by both parties**.

Property management services only can be provided **under the supervision of a designated broker**. While **real estate licensees are permitted to sign property management agreements**, the licensee only can only provide property management services if this service is offered by their employing broker.

KEY IDEAS TO REMEMBER:

- The agreement must have a set starting and ending date.
- Unlike a listing agreement, a property management agreement can have an automatic renewal provision as long as a 30-day out is provided.
- The agreement should specify how rent will be collected, what the timeframe is for notices to be provided to tenants and who will hold the security deposits – the owner or the property manager.

- The property management agreement should specify what reports a property manager will provide the owner, and how often they will be provided.
- A property management agreement **WOULD NOT** include an annual budget.

Property managements are custodians for the property. It is their responsibility to make the property as profitable as possible for as long as property.

Trust Accounts

Employing brokerages that offer property management **MUST** have a broker's trust account to hold client and tenant funds. Whenever a licensee or broker receives client funds, they must be deposited in the trust account **within three business days**.

Anyone who works for the brokerage, licensed or unlicensed, can be a signatory on the trust account. Property owners **NEVER** can be a signatory, primarily because there usually is more than one owner's money in the account.

Finder's Fees

It is illegal in Arizona to compensate any unlicensed individual for anything dealing with real estate **with the exception of finder's fees on rentals**. A property owner or property manager can offer finder's fees for tenants who refer new tenants. However, this only can be given as a **credit towards or reduction in** the tenant's monthly rent.

The maximum finder's fee allowed by statute is $400 and there is no statutory limit on how many finder's fees an individual tenant can receive.

Chapter 20
Property Insurance and Warranties

This is an extremely lightly tested chapter and there only are a few concepts to know.

Residential Property Insurance and Warranties
KEY IDEAS TO REMEMBER:
- The primary insurance on real property is hazard insurance.
  - o Lenders require hazard insurance to protect their collateral.
  - o The lender generally is listed as a "loss payee" – the first party to be paid when a major claim is filed.
  - o The homeowner generally is an "additional insured" – the second party to be paid.
- The AAR purchase contract requires sellers to provide buyers with an Insurance Claims History.
  - o Lexis/Nexis maintains the master database.
  - o The report either is for the last five years or however long the seller owned the property, which is less.
- Home warranties are separate from hazard insurance and cover issues with the electric, plumbing, built-in appliances and mechanical systems.

Business Insurance

Employing brokerages generally purchase **Errors and Omissions insurance.** E&O insurance is similar to **malpractice insurance for doctors**.

KEY IDEAS TO REMEMBER:
- E&O insurance will cover misrepresentation (unintentional errors).
- E&O insurance WILL NOT cover fraud (intentional errors) or violations of law such as Fair Housing or Sherman Anti-Trust violations.

Some brokers or licensees also purchase an **umbrella policy**, which provides coverage beyond the standard E&O coverage.

Chapter 21
Appraisal

Like the previous chapter, appraisals are a lightly tested topic. Unlike property insurance, however, these is a small avalanche of vocabulary terms and concepts that could appear on the real estate exam.

An **appraisal** is an estimate or opinion of value, based on data as of a set date known as the **effective date**.

Value

KEY IDEAS TO REMEMBER:
- Market value is what the property should sell for in a perfect world. This is determined by the appraiser as an estimate or opinion of value.
- Market price is what buyer and seller actually agreed to – the sales price.

There are four components to value – **demand, utility, scarcity and transferability.** The more demand there is for a property, the more useful it is, the scarcer it is and the more easily transferable it is, the more value it has.

Square Footage
- **Livable square footage –** all heated and cooled spaces
- **Under roof square footage –** everything under the roof, including the garage
- **Residential square footage is measured from the exterior**
- **Commercial square footage is measured from the interior for leases**

Appraisal Concepts
The good news is you'll never be asked to differentiate between substitution, for example, and conformity. Many of these concepts are similar but the questions should give you clearly correct and incorrect options.

- **Highest and best use** – the first thing an appraiser looks at, this is a property's most profitable, feasible and legal use. A house in an area zoned industrial would be a negative example of highest and best use.
- **Substitution** – the idea a buyer will not pay more for one property than for a substantially equal property. 18-inch title may look nicer than 13-inch title, but your average buyer won't pay more for the larger tile.
- **Anticipation** – the idea that a future even will either positively or negatively impact property values in an area. Think of the tech companies coming to Goodyear and the likely increase in values stemming from new jobs.
- **Supply and demand** – basic economics. The more the demand and/or the less the supply, the more the value and vice versa.
- **Contribution** – the idea that an improvement's value only is what value it adds to a property's overall value. For example, in the Phoenix area, even if you spend $50,000 on a pool, it only will add about $8,000 - $10,000 to the home's value.
- **Plottage increment/Assemblage** – the whole is worth more than the sum of the parts. Combining two or more lots to create a parcel of higher value than the sum of the current parcels' value.
- **Direction growth** – in what direction is an area growing, toward the suburbs or back toward downtown? This is tied into demand.
- **Orientation** – what direction does the house face? North-south exposures in the Phoenix area usually have more value than east-west exposures.
- **Unearned increment** – increases of value that take place without the owner having done anything to earn it. Businesses near Westgate in Glendale that predate Westgate and the Arizona Cardinals' stadium have experienced this.
- **Economic life** – the length of time an improvement (read: building) should add value to a parcel of land.
- **Excess land** – acreage or land that may not be part of the appraisal but has to be considered because, if used, it can add value to the property.

Appraisal Approaches

Sales Comparison/Market Data Approach
The **sales comparison approach** is driven by comps – properties comparable to the subject property. This also is the **only** approach that can be used for vacant land.

The subject property – the property being appraised – never is adjusted. Instead, the value of the comps is adjusted to artificially turn them into similar properties to the subject.

KEY IDEAS TO REMEMBER:
- If the subject property is better, add value to the comparable.
- If the comparable property is better, subtract value from the comparable.

Cost Approach

The **cost approach** involves estimating the construction cost of the subject property and then artificially lowering or **depreciating** that value to reflect current condition. The cost approach is used most often **when comps aren't available** – flood- or fire-damaged homes, historic homes, schools, churches, etc.

- **First,** the appraiser estimates the value of the land using the market approach.
- **Next,** the appraiser estimates construction value in one of two ways:
    - **Replacement value** – this is the cost of replacing the building using current materials and methods. This is for any kind of standard property.
    - **Reproduction value** – this is the cost of creating an exact replica of the building using time-appropriate materials. This would be for a historic home or similar property.
- **Third,** the appraiser artificially depreciates the replacement or reproduction value for different factors. These can be **curable** or **incurable**, depending on whether corrections can be made.
    - **Physical depreciation** – basic wear and tear, also known as **deferred maintenance**. The house needs new paint, new carpet, etc. This almost always is curable.
    - **Functional obsolescence** – something about the house makes it less than ideal from a functional standpoint. A five-bedroom house with only one bathroom has functional obsolescence as morning showers will take forever. Function obsolescence can be either curable or incurable.
    - **Economic obsolescence** – this always is off the property and is always incurable. Think of properties backing to shopping centers or landfills or in the flight path of an Air Force base.
- **Lastly,** the appraiser adds the depreciated construction value to the land value to determine the final appraised value.

Income Approach

The **income approach** only is possible on income-producing properties. The appraiser will estimate the **net operating income** (see below) for a property and divide that NOI by the expected **capitalization rate** for the area. The result is the appraised market value.

$$\text{NOI} \div \text{Cap rate} = \text{Appraised Value via Income Approach}$$

Reconciliation

If an appraiser uses more than one approach, they never will average the valuations from the different approaches. Instead, the appraiser will **reconcile** the different values **(reconciliation)**, weighting each appropriately.

Financial Analysis

There are several basic formulas to measure investment performance – **cap rate**, **before tax cash flow** and **cash on cash return**, also known as **return on equity**.

Net Operating Income

Let's start with an apartment building. Imagine a scenario where every tenant pays their rent on time, no one bounces a check and there never are any vacancies. In this situation, the owner would be collecting the maximum rent possible every year. We call this hypothetical number the **projected** or **potential gross income**.

You and I both know that no such property exists. There always are going to be vacancies or bad debts or credit losses in a given year. So, we now will subtract the estimated **vacancies and credit losses** from the projected gross income. This gives us a more realistic income number, the **effective gross income**.

Of course, it costs money to operate a building, so we are going to subtract those **operating expenses** from the effective gross income. What's left is our **net operating income** or **NOI**.

Operating Expenses

Not all operating expenses are created equally. For our purposes, we only are going to subtract those operating expenses which are building specific – **property taxes**, **insurance**, **maintenance** and **management**. We won't include investor-specific operating expenses such as **depreciation**, **income taxes**, **debt service** and **improvements**.

Capitalization Rate

As we discussed in the income section of appraisals, when we divide the net operating income by the value of the property, we get the **capitalization** or **cap rate** or **rate of return** for the property. Same formula, just solving for the cap rate instead of the value.

$$\text{NOI} \div \text{Value} = \text{Capitalization (Cap) Rate}$$

Leverage

Leverage is the financial art of spending other people's money. Or, to paraphrase the poets Naughty by Nature, leverage means you're down with OPM.

Before Tax Cash Flow

While we don't include debt service as a general operating expense because not all investors use leverage, for those who do borrow to invest, the debt service is a very real cost. That's where **before tax cash flow** comes in. The before tax cash flow is the net operating income less the debt service – the annual interest to be paid.

$$\text{Before Tax Cash Flow} = \text{NOI} - \text{Debt Service}$$

Return on Equity/Cash on Cash Return

Just as the cap rate reflects the return an investor can expect based on the cash they've spent – in that case, the full purchase price, the **cash on cash return** or **return on equity** reflects the return on the cash the investor is spending out of pocket on the investment. We don't care about the full purchase price, only the amount of the money the investor's spending out of pocket.

$$\text{Before Tax Cash Flow} \div \$\$ \text{ Out of Pocket} = \text{Cash on Cash Return}$$

Licensing

Appraisers must be licensed per **FIRREA (Financial Institution Reform, Recovery and Enforcement Act.)** Any question with FIRREA, there is your answer. Only a licensed appraiser can perform appraisals.

- **Licensed residential appraisers** can appraise residential properties (one to four units) with sales prices under $1,000,000.
- **Certified residential appraisers** can appraise any residential property.
- **Certified general appraisers** can appraise any type of property.

Appraisers use the **Uniform Residential Appraisal Report**, the form and format approved by Fannie Mae and Freddie Mac.

Competitive Market Analysis

Real estate licensees cannot perform appraisals but we can perform **competitive market analyses (CMAs.)** Appraisers only look at sold properties for their appraisal. For a CMA, a licensee would look at both Active and Sold properties in the MLS.

KEY IDEA TO REMEMBER:

- Real estate licensees can never say that what they are providing is an appraisal. Home valuation, CMA or comps are acceptable terms.

Broker Price Opinions

A **broker price opinion** is a mini-appraisal, never referred to as an appraisal but similar in scope, that lenders would order for bank owned homes before putting them on the market for resale. Make sure you know **all compensation – including compensation for broker price opinions – is paid to the employing broker.**

Appraisal Process

When a lender orders an appraisal for a residential property, they can't call an appraiser directly. Instead, the lender contacts an **appraisal management company**, who will assign one of their affiliated appraisers to work the property.

- **Drive-by appraisal** – just what it sounds like, the appraiser will drive by the subject property but usually will not step inside the property to verify.
- **Desktop appraisal** – the appraiser relies on the multiple listing service and other sources and never leaves the office to complete the appraisal.
- **Automated Valuation Models** – think Zillow's "zestimates." Large swaths of properties are lumped together and values averaged to determine "value".

Chapter 22
Primary and Secondary Markets and Financing Concepts

In this section, we will review the primary and secondary mortgage markets, the role of the Federal Reserve and different types of loan programs.

Primary Market

When a buyer needs a loan to purchase a home, they would go to a **primary market** lender. These include mortgage bankers, mortgage brokers, banks, credit unions, etc.

The three main functions of the primary market are **origination, underwriting** and **servicing**. Origination is all the work performed to put together the loan package. That package then is delivered to the underwriters, who determine whether the borrower is credit worthy. Lastly, after the loan is made, a bank or other entity will service the loan – send statements, collect payments, etc.

KEY IDEAS TO REMEMBER:
- **Lenders often charge borrowers origination or underwriting fees.**
- **Servicing companies charge the primary market lender fees for servicing the loan after it has been made.**
- **Lenders make their profit on origination and servicing.**
- **Primary market loans are referred to as "paper".**

Secondary Market

Loans, or paper, are bought and sold on the **secondary market**. The main players in the secondary market are **private investors, foreign governments** and three entities – **Fannie Mae, Ginnie Mae** and **Freddie Mac**.

Fannie Mae (Federal National Mortgage Association/FNMA)

KEY IDEAS TO REMEMBER:
- Fannie Mae is the largest player on the secondary market.
- Fannie Mae is government sponsored, NOT government owned.
- Fannie Mae buys loans, bundles large numbers of loans together through securitization and sells the mortgage-backed securities.

Ginnie Mae (Government National Mortgage Association)

KEY IDEAS TO REMEMBER:
- Ginnie Mae (GNMA) is government owned.
- Ginnie Mae only purchases FHA and VA loans. Because of this, Ginnie Mae guarantees the loans it re-sells. Specifically, Ginnie Mae guarantees payment of principal and interest to investors.
- Like Fannie Mae, Ginnie Mae buys loans in bulk, bundles these loans through securitization and sells the mortgage-backed securities.
- Purchases of Ginnie Mae loan bundles receive a pass-through certificate.
- Ginnie Mae also purchases low- and moderate-income loans.

Freddie Mac (Federal Home Loan Mortgage Corporation)

Freddie Mac rarely is tested. If you do see questions, the main thing to know about Freddie Mac is that it, like Fannie Mae, is **government sponsored.**

Estoppel Certificate

When loans are sold on the secondary market, the investor receives an **estoppel certificate** that verifies the terms of the loan being purchased.

Federal Reserve

The role of the **Federal Reserve** is to promote economic growth while also limiting inflation. The key phrase with the Federal Reserve is **open market operations**. The Fed sets the discount or fed funds rate, which is the rate the Fed charges member banks to borrow money. The Fed also can raise and lower banks' reserve requirement – how much money each bank needs on hand at the end of the banking day – and also can buy or sell government securities.

Loan Types

There are several types of loans whose names reflect either their purpose or the way the loans are paid back.

- **Open End loan** – a loan where the borrower can take multiple draws off of the same loan. This would be a home equity line of credit or construction loan.
- **Blanket loan** – a loan covering more than one parcel of real estate. These loans include a **release clause**. When a developer builds a house on one parcel, for example, they would pay a lump sum to the bank and that parcel would be released as collateral through the release clause.
- **Reverse mortgage** – this loan, available to borrowers 62 and over, is called a reverse mortgage because it is the bank making payments to the borrower based on the equity in their property. This loan remains in effect until the borrower dies, abandons the property or relocates, at which point the money paid and interest is due.
- **Interest only loan** – the borrower is paying interest only every month, with not a cent going to principal. The full principal balance is due at the end of the loan.
- **Balloon payment** – the borrower makes monthly payments but has a much larger, balloon payment due at the end of the loan term.
- **Amortized loan** – the borrower makes the same payment every month, paying both principal and interest and ending the loan with zero principal due.
- **Budget loan** – still an amortized loan, except the borrower also is paying 1/12 of their property taxes and insurance. This often is known as a PITI payment – principal, interest, taxes and insurance.
- **Package loan** – a loan for both real and personal property. Think of a loan for a time share, where both the unit and the furnishings are included.
- **Private investor/hard money** – loans for those whose credit or other factors may not allow them to qualify for a traditional loan. These usually have far higher interest rates than traditional loans.

Adjustable Rate/Variable Rate Loans

A **fixed rate** loan is a loan where the interest rate remains the same for the life of the loan. This interest rate is fixed during the escrow period before closing using a **rate lock** – just as it sounds, the rate now is locked.

An **adjustable rate loan** is a loan where the interest rate floats or adjusts over time. There are three components to an adjustable rate loan, or ARM.

Index

The interest rate is tied to a cost of living **index**. As the index fluctuates, so does the interest rate on the loan.

Margin

The **margin** is the percentage added to the index to give the final interest rate and is pure profit for the lender. This margin remains the same for the life of the loan.

Caps

The **loan cap** limits how much the rate can increase during each adjustment period and for the life of a loan. A 2/6 cap, for example, would mean the interest rate cannot increase by more than two percent each adjustment cycle and cannot increase more than six percent over the life of the loan.

Construction Loans

There are three types of loans associated with new construction – the **construction loan** itself, a **gap** or **bridge** loan, and the **permanent** or **take out** loan.

Construction Loan

This is used during the construction phase of a real estate project. The developer can take multiple draws off the same loan and no repayment is needed until a **certificate of occupancy** has been issued. At that point, the loan is due in full. Lenders may require a **performance bond**, basically like a bail bond, so if the developer goes under, the bank will get repaid by the surety company.

Permanent/Take Out Loan

The **take out** loan is the developer's permanent financing. It's called a take out loan because it "takes out" any other construction loans the developer has.

Gap/Bridge Loan

Though the construction loan is due in full when the certificate of occupancy has been issued, depending on the project, the developer may not be able to obtain permanent financing immediately. Instead, they will get a **gap** or **bridge** loan that, as it sounds, bridges the gap between the construction and take out loans.

Seller Financing

Seller financing is any situation in which the seller acts as the lender. Instead of going to a bank, the buyer will give the seller a promissory note and sign either a mortgage or deed of trust. The seller is agreeing to take payments of principal and interest over time rather than getting the fill proceeds immediately.

Loan Assumption

A **loan assumption** is when the buyer takes over the seller's loan. This can be done with or without **novation**.

Novation

Novation is the substitution of one borrower for another. On a loan assumption **with novation**, the seller no longer is legally liable for the original loan. **Without novation**, the seller still is legally liable even though the buyer has taken over the payments.

Wraparound Loan

When we talk about seller financing, the assumption is the seller owns the property free and clear. But that's not always the case. On a **wraparound loan**, the seller has a loan on the property already and then creates or "wraps" a new loan around the original loan. The buyer then makes one payment based on this new loan.

An **account servicing** company usually is hired to handle payments and keep the paperwork. The servicing company will take the buyer's payments and split it into two checks – one goes to the seller's original lender and the second, for the difference in interest between the two loans, goes to the seller.

Loan Clauses and Vocabulary

There are a handful of different clauses that can be included within the loan.

- **Acceleration clause** – if the borrower falls behind on their payments, in other words is in default, this clause says the lender can accelerate the due date for the loan and make the entire loan due in full immediately.

- **Alienation clause** – this is a "due on sale" clause. If the seller sells the property, the entire loan balance is due immediately. This also is known as a **non-assumption clause**, and protects the lender by preventing loan assumptions.

- **Defeasance clause** – this clause "defeats" the lender's interest in a property. When a mortgage or deed of trust is paid in full, the defeasance clause requires the lender to formally release their interest within 30 days.

- **Subordination clause** – this allows a lien to drop in priority. If a borrower gets both a traditional loan and seller financing to purchase a property, there will be a subordination clause that says the traditional loan will be in first position no matter what.

- **Prepayment penalty** – if the borrower pays the loan off before some set time period, they will have to pay an additional penalty. Loans without prepayment penalties have an **"or more" clause**, which allows the borrower to pay the minimum payment up to the full amount due any month they choose.

- **Non-disturbance clause** – this is included in a lease and says the lease will remain in effect even if the owner defaults on their loan and is foreclosed on.

- **Non-recourse loan** – a loan where the lender has no ability to pursue a deficiency balance after default. Reverse mortgages are non-recourse loans because, if the house is worth less than the amount paid on the loan, the lender cannot pursue the estate for the extra money owed.

Chapter 23
Residential and Commercial Financing

There are four main residential loan programs you will need to know for the real estate test – **FHA, VA, USDA** and **conventional**. This section also covers commercial financing terminology and two laws that are vital in real estate lending, **Regulation Z** and **RESPA**.

Loan to Value Ratio

The **loan to value ratio** is the percentage of the sales price that has been borrowed with the loan. For example, a loan with a 20 percent down payment has an 80% LTV.

FHA Financing

FHA loans are **insured** by the Federal Housing Administration. If a buyer wants to get an FHA loan, they go to a primary market lender – not FHA. FHA loans are for owner-occupied residential properties (one to four units). A borrower does not need to be a U.S. citizen to get an FHA loan.

FHA loans:
- Are insured, not guaranteed
- Require a minimum down payment of 3.5 percent (96.5% LTV)
- Include MIP or UFMIP – a mortgage insurance premium, which is an upfront (thus the UF) and monthly fee.
- Are subject to an appraisal
    - o   FHA appraisals attach to the property for 120 days
- Have a maximum loan amount, set by Congress
- Are fully assumable and never have a pre-payment penalty
- Allow for seller contributions up to 6 percent of the sales price
- Require an FHA Amendatory Clause, which says the borrower will get their earnest deposit back if the property doesn't appraise

Borrowers receive a **conditional commitment**, which says the loan will be funded subject to an appraisal and minimum habitability standards. Lenders who meet FHA requirements to write these loans are known as **direct endorsement lenders**.

VA Financing

VA loans are **guaranteed** by the Veterans Administration. A servicemember would need to have served for two years (90 days in an active war zone) and received an honorable discharge to be eligible. Like FHA loans, VA loans are for owner-occupied residential properties (one to four units).

Upon eligibility, the servicemember received an **entitlement**, which is set by Congress. When a servicemember purchases a property, 25 percent of the sales price is deducted from the entitlement. Servicemembers are able to use that excess entitlement – whatever amount remains - to buy a second house under certain circumstances, such as being transferred to a new base.

VA loans:
- Are guaranteed, not insured
- Have a maximum loan amount set be Congress (this will change in 2020)
    - The maximum loan amount is four times the veterans' entitlement
- Can be made with zero down (100% LTV)
- Do not require either MIP or Private Mortgage Insurance, but do include a one-time funding fee.
    - The amount of the funding fee varies depending on terms of service and the number of times the VA benefit has been used.
- Are subject to an appraisal, known as a Certificate of Reasonable Value
- Are fully assumable and never have a pre-payment penalty
    - Veterans and non-veterans alike can assume VA loans. If a veteran assumes the loan, the original borrower gets their full entitlement back. If a non-veteran assumes the loan, the original borrower will not get their entitlement back until the loan is closed out via a new sale or refinance
- Can have points paid by either buyer or seller

Conventional Loans

Compared to FHA and VA loans, there are very few restrictions on **conventional loans**. While most of us think of conventional loans as requiring 20 percent down, that percentage can vary depending on the lender and the loan program. Conventional loans can be used for both owner-occupied and investment properties and are subject to the property appraising for at least the loan amount.

KEY IDEAS TO REMEMBER:

- Conventional loans made with less than 20% down (LTV higher than 80%) require private mortgage insurance.
- Borrowers can request the PMI be removed once they reach 80% LTV and the lender MUST remove the PMI when the loan is at 78% LTV.

Conforming conventional loans are loans that meet Fannie Mae and Freddie Mac underwriting standards. In other words, these are loans Fannie or Freddie would buy.

Loans that do not meet Fannie and Freddie underwriting standards are called **non-conforming loans**. Loans can be non-conforming because of the **size of the loan (jumbo loans)** or the **creditworthiness of the borrower (subprime loans).**

USDA Financing

USDA financing is a new additional to the curriculum. USDA loans provide zero down financing for low- to moderate-income borrowers in rural areas.

Regulation Z/RESPA

The **Truth in Lending Act (Regulation Z)** and the **Real Estate Settlement Procedures Act (RESPA)** often are confusing because the differences between the two are thin. But there's a fairly easy way to keep the two of them separate. Also, keep in mind, most test questions won't ask you to know whether any particular charge should fall under Reg Z or RESPA.

KEY IDEA TO REMEMBER:
- Both Reg Z and RESPA are regulated by the Consumer Financial Protection Bureau (CFPB).

Truth in Lending Act/Regulation Z

The Truth in Lending Act requires the **full disclosure of all costs associated with obtaining credit**. This applies not just to real estate but to any type of loan, including credit cards – any loan **with more than four payments where interest is charged**.

The key to Reg Z is **trigger terms**. Think numbers. If the question involves numbers of some sort and disclosure, it's almost certainly a Reg Z question. The basic idea is if any trigger term – number – dealing with the costs of obtaining a loan is disclosed, **all numbers have to be disclosed**.

Trigger terms include **interest rate, down payment, monthly payment, origination and underwriting fees** and the **annual percentage rate.**

KEY IDEA TO REMEMBER:
- The annual percentage rate is all the costs of the loan – interest, origination fees, points, doc fees – all rolled into one percentage number. The APR always will be higher than the interest rate on the loan.

If a lender advertises a loan requiring $1,000 down or a $700 monthly payment, the lender now has to disclose all the conditions that led to those numbers – loan type, loan term, sales price, interest rate, points, origination fee, etc.

There only are two items in Reg Z that we deal with that don't deal with numbers:

- Borrowers receive a three-day rescission period when they refinance their personal residence.
- An appraiser's fee cannot be contingent upon the appraisal hitting the number (i.e., the appraiser only gets paid if the property appraises for the sales price.)

Real Estate Settlement Procedures Act (RESPA)

The Real Estate Settlement Procedures Act (RESPA) **requires the full disclosure of all settlement or closing costs**. While there are numbers associated with RESPA – escrow fees, title fees, etc. – the key to RESPA are the disclosures and prohibitions.

Within **three days of loan application**, a borrower must receive both a **Loan Estimate (a good faith estimate)** and a **booklet, Your Home Loan Toolkit.**

Within **three days before loan consummation (signing loan docs)**, the borrower must receive a **Closing Disclosure**. This disclosure replaced the old HUD-1 form.

These forms are required by the **Truth in Lending/RESPA Integrated Disclosure rule**, passed as part of the Dodd-Frank Act after the mortgage meltdown.

There are other deadlines contained within RESPA and the later TRID rule, but the above two are the ones you will need to know.

RESPA also **prohibits kickbacks** and **referral fees**. Kickbacks and referral fees are anything of value given in exchange for the referral of business. Brokerages can have **Affiliated Business Arrangements**, either with other companies the brokerage owner also owns or so-called preferred vendors. These must be disclosed in writing to all parties and the broker cannot require its clients to use these companies.

If lenders had their way, they would want to collect years' worth of property taxes and insurance as part of the closing. RESPA, however, says the lender can **only collect two months of property taxes and insurance** at closing to start the impound account.

Homeowners associations also usually require at least two months' payment in advance.

Loan Fees and Interest Rates

A **discount point** is a percentage paid up front by a borrower to reduce their interest rate. For testing purposes, a discount point is defined as **1 percent of the loan amount** paid up front at closing to reduce the interest rate by **1/8 of one percent**

For example, if Fred is getting a $200,000 loan at 5 percent interest, he can pay 1 percent of the loan amount – $2,000 – to reduce his interest rate to 4 7/8 percent.

Don't worry about how points work in real life in terms of interest reductions, just remember 1 percent of the loan amount to reduce the interest rate 1/8 of a percent.

Origination and **underwriting fees** are exactly what they sound like – fees charged by a lender for **origination** and **underwriting**.

Loan Qualifications

To qualify a borrower, lenders will look at a number of factors – income, debt, FICO and other credit scores, cash reserves, etc.

Front End/Back End Ratios

The **front end** or **income ratio** is the borrower's potential PITI payment (principal, interest, taxes and insurance) divided by the borrower's gross monthly income.

The **back end** or **debt ratio** is the borrower's total monthly debt obligation (the new loan payment, auto loans, credit cards, student loans) divided by the borrower's gross monthly income.

Borrowers must qualify under both ratios for their loan.

PITI Payment ÷ Gross Monthly Income = Front End Ratio

Total Monthly Debt ÷ Gross Monthly Income = Back End Ratio

Commercial Financing

- **Small Business Administration (SBA) loans** – loans issued by the Small Business Administration to small business with very favorable terms.
- **Personal guarantee** – since many businesses getting loans are brand new, there is no track record on which the lender can rely. Instead, the lender will require a personal guarantee, making the business owner personally liable for the loan.
- **Yield maintenance** – this is a prepayment penalty on a commercial loan. These usually are far more punitive than residential prepayment penalties but can result in more favorable terms.
- **Basis points** – a basis point or BiP is shorthand for 1/100 of a percent. If an interest rate drops to 4.74% from 4/75%, we say it dropped by one basis point.
- **Debt coverage ratio** – a ratio reflecting anticipated income versus the debt service the business owner is carrying. The higher the ratio the better.

Chapter 24
Financing Documents

This section dealing with financing documents is brief and leads into next chapter's review of foreclosure.

Financing Theory

States fall roughly into two categories – **title theory** and **lien theory** – based on how the lender enforces repayment of their loan.

In **title theory** states, the **lender holds legal title** until the final payment is made. The **borrower holds equitable title**. Make no mistake, the borrower owns the property but the legal title remains in the lender's name.

In **lien theory** states, the **borrower holds legal title** to the property and the **lender places a lien** against the property. Remember, a lien is a financial encumbrance and a way for a creditor to make sure they are paid by their debtor.

While Arizona's placement can lead to long debates in the real estate classroom, for our purposes Arizona is a **lien theory** state. There is a law on the books in Arizona that prohibits lenders from holding legal title.

Loan Components

Most loans consist or two components – a **financing instrument** and a **security instrument**. The financing instrument comes in the form of a **promissory note**.

This promissory note, at its most basic, is a glorified IOU. It creates the borrowers' legal obligation to repay the loan. But the promissory note does not include the property's legal description and is not recorded.

The **security instrument** comes in the form of a **collateral loan document.** The collateral loan document allows the borrower to **hypothecate** their property – pledge the property as collateral while maintaining possession of it.

Mortgages vs. Deeds of Trust

Mortgages and **deeds of trust** both are examples of collateral lien documents. While Arizona is an exception to the rule, mortgages usually are used in lien theory states and deeds of trust usually are used in title theory states.

Mortgages

There are two parties to a mortgage, the borrower and the lender. The borrower is known as the **mortgagor** while the lender is the **mortgagee**.

KEY IDEA TO REMEMBER:

- The assignment of the "or" and "ee" in this case has NOTHING to do with the money being loaned. It's all about the collateral loan document, the mortgage itself. The borrower is giving the collateral loan document to the lender and thus is the mortgagor. The lender is receiving this loan document, the mortgage, from the borrower and thus is the mortgagee.

When a mortgage is paid in full, the lender will send and record a **satisfaction of mortgage**. This is required by the defeasance clause and must be completed within 30 days of the loan being satisfied.

Mortgages, incidentally, are extremely rare in Arizona. We have been using deeds of trust for nearly fifty years. But use of a mortgage remains possible if unlikely.

Deeds of Trust

There are three parties to a deed of trust – the borrower, the lender and a neutral third party selected by the lender. The borrower is the **trustor**, the lender is the **beneficiary** and the neutral third party is the **trustee**.

KEY IDEA TO REMEMBER:

- The borrower, or trustor, is giving the collateral loan document – the deed of trust to the lender. However, since in Arizona the lender can't hold this document, the lender then gives it to the trustee. The trustee holds this document for the benefit of the lender, the beneficiary.

About the trustee:
- The trustee is a third-party selected by the beneficiary.
- The trustee is **paid one-half of one percent of the loan amount** by the beneficiary.

- The trustee holds **bare legal** or **naked title**. Basically, the trustee has just enough legal interest in the property either to foreclose on the borrower or send a **deed of reconveyance** when the loan is paid in full.
- The trustee does not collect payments, send statements, etc. That is the job of the loan servicing company.
- The trustee acts solely upon instruction from the beneficiary.

The trustee is a lot like the movie character Beetlejuice. You'll never know he's there until the beneficiary calls his name three times. But when the beneficiary does call on the trustee, things are going to happen.

Agreement for Sale/Land Contract

An **agreement for sale** is another version of seller financing. Agreements for sale commonly are known as land contracts because they commonly (but not exclusively) are used on the sale of land.

On an agreement for sale, the promissory note and collateral loan document are wrapped into the same instrument rather than existing separately. The seller on a land contract is known as the **vendor**, while the buyer is the **vendee**. The vendor or seller **holds legal title** to the property until the final payment is made.

Chapter 25
Deed of Trust Foreclosure

Despite this section's name, we also will review mortgage foreclosures and forfeitures on agreements for sale.

Non-Judicial Foreclosure

Non-judicial foreclosure is the process used most commonly with deeds of trust, which means this is what we see in Arizona nearly exclusively. Lenders **have the option to judicially foreclose**, **even on a deed of trust**, but rarely will.

This is the timeline on a non-judicial foreclosure:

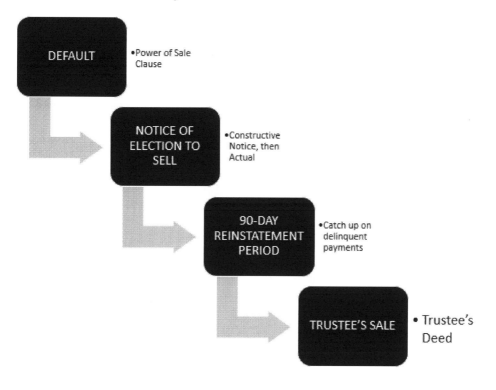

Power of Sale Clause

The key to non-judicial foreclosure is the **power of sale clause**. This clause gives the **trustee** the legal authority – the power – to sell a property when the borrower falls into default.

KEY IDEAS TO REMEMBER:
- The **borrower authorizes** the power of sale clause when they sign their loan documents.
- The **lender or beneficiary initiates** use of the power of sale clause when the borrower is in default.
- The **power of sale clause empowers the trustee** to sell the property.

Order of Notice/Reinstatement

The trustee, once ordered by the beneficiary to take action, first will prepare a **notice of election to sell** or **notice of sale**. This notice first is recorded with the county recorder's office. Then, within five days, the notice has to be sent to the borrower via process server or certified mail.

The order of notice, then, is **constructive** first – the recording – then **actual** – the physical notice being given to the borrower.

Once this notice is given, the clock starts on a **90-day reinstatement period**. Reinstating a loan means playing catch up – paying the delinquent balance as well as the trustee's fees. If the borrower catches up on payments, the foreclosure process stops.

KEY IDEAS TO REMEMBER:
- When dealing with foreclosure, watch for key words. If you see either "reinstate" or "reinstatement", these terms refer ONLY to non-judicial foreclosure and deeds of trust.

Trustee's Sale

At the end of the 90-day reinstatement period, the trustee will hold a **trustee's sale**. Highest bid wins and the full winning bid is due in cleared funds by 5 p.m. the day after the sale. If the borrower still is on the property, the winning bidder can have them forcibly evicted by an officer of the court, meaning the sheriff.

The winner of the trustee's sale receives a **trustee's deed**, which is one version of a bargain and sale deed.

Full Credit Bid

If the lender is not going to receive enough in proceeds from the trustee's sale, it would enter a **full credit bid**. Basically, the lender bids the amount of their loan and becomes the new owner of the property. Once that takes place, the property now is referred to as an **REO – real estate owned**. In other words, a bank-owned home.

Judicial Foreclosure

Judicial foreclosure is used in states that use **mortgages**. It is an incredibly slow, expensive, time-consuming process which is why, while it can be used in Arizona for a deed of trust, it's extremely rare to see.

Acceleration Clause

The key to judicial foreclosure is the **acceleration clause**. When a borrower on a mortgage is in default, the lender will use the acceleration clause to call the full loan amount due immediately. Unlike non-judicial foreclosure, there is no opportunity for a borrower to catch up on missed payments alone.

Notice of Default/Foreclosure Action

The lender will record and send the borrower a **notice of default**, notifying them that their full loan now is due. Then the lender will go to court and file a lawsuit called a **foreclosure action**.

From here, we wait.

Equitable Period of Redemption

From the time the foreclosure action is filed to the sheriff's sale, the borrower has what we call an **equitable period of redemption**. There's no time frame on how long this period can be. It depends on the court calendar. At the height of the housing crisis, in Illinois the equitable period of redemption was two to four years. In New York and New Jersey, it extended closer to five to seven years.

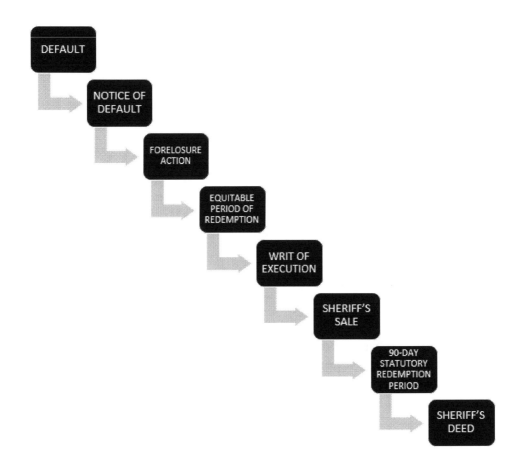

Writ of Execution/Sheriff's Sale

The equitable period of redemption ends when the court issues a **writ of execution.** This writ allows an officer of the court – the sheriff – to hold a **sheriff's sale**. Like the trustee's sale, this is an auction where the highest bid wins. Unlike the trustee's sale, the winner of a sheriff's sale does not get immediate ownership of the property.

The winner of the sheriff's sale receives a **certificate of sale**.

Statutory Redemption Period/Sheriff's Sale

In Arizona, borrowers have a **90-day redemption period after the sale**, during which they still can redeem their loan. Only after this statutory redemption period does the winning bidder of the sheriff's sale receive a sheriff's deed to the property.

KEY IDEAS TO REMEMBER:
- The key term on a judicial foreclosure is redemption. If you see either "redeem" or "redemption," these refer strictly to mortgages and judicial foreclosure.
  - Redeem or redemption – judicial foreclosure. Reinstate or reinstatement – non-judicial foreclosure.

Deficiency Judgments

If the lender does not receive the amount of the loan through the foreclosure sale, the lender can pursue a **deficiency judgment** – a second court filing where the lender seeks a judgment against the property owner for the remaining portion of the loan balance.

Anti-Deficiency Protection

Arizona is one of several states with **anti-deficiency protection**. Anti-deficiency protection applies to **residential properties**, **one or two units** sitting on **2½ acres or fewer**. Also, the loan must be a **purchase money loan** – either used for the purchase of the property or, in certain circumstances, for an improvement to the property (for example, a loan for a new pool.)

Alternatives to Foreclosure

Deeds in Lieu of Foreclosure

A **deed in lieu of foreclosure** is the real estate equivalent of taking your car back to the dealership and giving back the keys. The lender agrees to take ownership of the property – take back the deed – in lieu of foreclosing on a delinquent borrower.

If you remember the term "cash for keys," where borrowers received a check from the lender in exchange for not trashing the house, those were deeds in lieu of foreclosure.

Forbearance

Forbearance takes place when the lender elects not to foreclose on a delinquent borrower. For example, it may make more sense for the lender to allow the owner of a $2 million property continue living in the house even without making payments rather than leave the property vacant and ready to be vandalized.

Short Sale

A **short sale** is when the lender agrees to accept a lower sale price for a property than what the lender is owed.

Forfeiture – Agreements for Sale

As a reminder, an **agreement for sale** is a method of seller financing where the seller or vendor sells the property on installment to a buyer or vendee but holds the legal title until the final payment is made.

When a buyer defaults on an agreement for sale, they enter the **forfeiture** process. If they don't catch up on their delinquent payments, they will forfeit their rights of ownership back to the seller.

The amount of time a buyer has to cure their default depends on the **equity** they have in the property – the percentage of the purchase price the buyer already has paid the seller. The higher the percentage, the more time the buyer has.

You **do not** need to know the specific forfeiture timeframes for the test.

Chapter 26
Disclosure/Consumer Protection

Disclosure is a topic that comes up in multiple different places, from environmental and water issues to the definitions of material facts and material defects. This section contains a handful of disclosure topics along with consumer protection laws.

As a general rule, licensees need to take care with client's **personal identifying information** to help prevent **identity theft**. Documents contains such information – bank statements, credit reports, even the purchase contract – need to be kept in a secure area. When disposing of these documents, they should either be shredded or burned.

While personal identifying information is not tied directly to **wire fraud**, we need to make sure our clients understand not to follow any wiring instructions they receive via e-mail without first verifying the sender.

Do Not Call List
The **Do Not Call Registry** is a national database where consumers register their phone numbers to prevent marketing calls. We won't discuss how effective this really is, just that you need to know it for the test. Licensees cannot call phone numbers they see either on For Sale by Owner signs, expired listings or even Zillow without scrubbing that phone number against the Do Not Call List.

In addition to the national list, brokerages need to maintain an internal list.

Penalties
The fine for violating the **Do Not Call** laws is up to **$40,654 per offense**.

Exceptions
If a new customer makes an inquiry of you and provides their phone number, you have **up to three months** to follow up with them. If you or your brokerage has worked with a client in the past, in other words, you have an **established business relationship** with the client, you can contact them for **up to 18 months**.

CAN-SPAM Act

The **CAN-SPAM Act** deals with e-mail marketing. Subject lines cannot be deceptive, the e-mails have to detail that they are advertisements, etc.

Opt Out

All marketing e-mails **must include a one-step opt out or unsubscribe option**. We can't make people jump through multiple hoops to unsubscribe from an e-mail.

Penalties

The fine for violating the CAN-SPAM Act is **$16,000 per e-mail offense**.

Disclosures – Airports

The presence of an airport in the vicinity of a property is a **material fact** that must be disclosed. This applies to public, private and military airports.

In Arizona, there are additional disclosure requirements for properties in the "territory in the vicinity of a military airport" or "territory in the vicinity of an ancillary military facility" or along a military training route. Each of Arizona's military airports has a defined territorial zone, for which maps can be found on the Arizona State Land Department websites. Licensees are required to ensure that buyers have received additional disclosures about the proximity of these military bases.

Fix and Flips

In Arizona, any repairs or renovations in excess of $1,000 require the use of a licensed contractor. Contractors are registered with the **Registrar of Contractors**. The exception is, a property owner **does not** have to use a contractor **if they are going to reside in the property for at least one year after the work is complete**.

What this means is, for investors intending to **fix and flip** properties, **a contractor absolutely is require**d if the cost of the work is more than $1,000 because they will not be occupying the property. Most of us likely know of investors and others who didn't follow this law, but don't let that get in the way of knowing what the law says.

Builders' Requirements

Builders are required to provide buyers with a **two-year warranty**.

Chapter 27
Cooperative Nature of Real Estate

Professional Boards and Associations

The **National Association of REALTORS** is the largest real-estate trade organization in the world and one of the largest trade organizations in the United States. Membership is optional, unless your employing broker is a member of NAR.

When you join NAR, you do so through both the state association – the **Arizona Association of REALTORS** – and a local board. Examples include the Tucson, Phoenix, West Maricopa, Verde Valley, Scottsdale, Flagstaff and Southeast Valley Associations of RELATORS.

KEY IDEAS TO REMEMBER:
- The purpose of the National Association of REALTORS is to promote professional ethics and standards.

All members of NAR voluntarily agree to abide by NAR's **Code of Ethics and Standards of Practice**. REALTORS are required to take continuing education classes about the code of ethics **every two years**.

Sherman Anti-Trust Act

The **Sherman Antitrust Act of 1890** was the first federal law that dealt with trusts – large corporations that often engaged in anti-competitive activities designed to hamper other's business interests and, by extension, harm the public.

Antitrust activities are anything that results in a lack of fair competition and trade among competing companies.

Price Fixing

You likely heard this a thousand times in class, but I will say it again. **THERE ARE NOT SET COMMISSION RATES. ALL COMMISSION RATES ARE FULLY NEGOTIABLE PER THE SHERMAN ANTI-TRUST ACT.**

If two or more licensees or brokers collude to set commission rates for a given area, this would be considered **price fixing** and is a violation of the Sherman Anti-Trust Act. In addition, if two or more property managers collude to set rental rates for a given area, this also would be considered price fixing.

NOTE: An individual brokerage CAN set its own commission schedule that all licensees working for that brokerage must follow. Office policies are fine. But working with other brokers to set commission rates is illegal.

Boycotts

We as licensees are required to work with all other brokerages unless it's not in our client's best interest not to so. A brokerage or brokerages cannot decide not to work with a given brokerage in hopes of driving that third broker out of business. That would be an illegal **boycott**.

Market/Territory Allocation

Two or more brokers cannot collude to divide territory, promising not to compete in each other's area. This harms the consumer by limiting competition and is illegal **market** or **territory allocation**.

Tie-In Agreements

A broker cannot attach a mandatory second agreement onto their employment agreement with a client. For example, if you help a buyer find a house, you cannot require them to sign an agreement that says they have to use you when they decide to sell. This would be an **illegal tie-in agreement**.

Penalties

Civil violations of the Sherman Anti-Trust Act could result in fines of triple the damages suffered by the plaintiff. Criminal violations can result in fines of up to $350,000 for individuals and $10 million for corporations.

Parties Related to a Real Estate Transaction

As we've already reviewed, contractors are licensed through the Registrar of Contractors. Mortgage loan originators are licensed through the state Department of Financial Institutions and also must be registered in the **National Mortgage Licensing System (NMLS).**

Home Inspectors

Home inspectors are licensed through the **Arizona Board of Technical registration.**

Pest Control (Termite) Inspectors

Pest control and termite inspectors are licensed through the **Pest Management Division** of the **Arizona Department of Agriculture**

Chapter 28
Real Estate Math

Before we start … breathe. Most students are filled with anxiety at the idea of real estate math. But the simple reality is, there are no complicated calculations here. Everything we do, and all that we will do, involves only addition, subtraction, multiplication and division.

That's all.

And even for percentage problems, which often cause the bulk of the confusion, there is a simple trick that will see you through.

DO NOT listen to those who tell you the math doesn't matter, that you can pass without getting a single math problem right. You need 75% to pass. Skip all of the math and you're starting at a 91%. That's just silly.

Lastly, keep in mind this is a review. Use these explanations, in combination with the materials you received in class, to see you through.

Ready? Here we go …

Prorations

The first question I'm asked whenever I teach this is whether we as real estate licensees are going to need to know how to this in real life. The answer, of course, is absolutely not! We have software and escrow folks for that.

Having said that, proration problems only involve four steps. Maybe it's because these problems often are paired with the ideas of debits and credits, who has to pay what, that they end up feeling harder than they are.

Here are the steps …

1. **Who owes what to whom?**

2. **What is the charge per day?**

3. **How many days are owed?**

4. **Multiply days by charge per day.**

That's it. That's all there is to it. Now let's look at some proration hacks.

First of all, when you get your scratch paper, draw yourself a quick 30-day calendar. If you at some point need a 31-day month, add the day.

1	2	3	4	5	6	7
8	9	10	11	12	13	14
15	16	17	18	19	20	21
22	23	24	25	26	27	28
29	30					

Keep in mind, this is one month of the year. You have to account for either the months before or months after depending on whether you are prorating a charge paid in advance or in arrears.

- **If the charge was paid in arrears, count the days UP the calendar from the COE date**
- **If the charge was paid in advance, count the days DOWN the calendar from the COE date**

There's no easy rule whether to include the COE in a count. On that, you just need to read the problem to see who is responsible for the proration that day.

Here are the other rules to keep in mind on prorations:

Step One – Who owes what?

- **If a charge was paid in advance, CREDIT THE SELLER and DEBIT THE BUYER.** (The buyer is reimbursing the seller).

- **If a charge was paid in arrears, DEBIT THE SELLER** and **CREDIT THE BUYER.** (The seller has to give the buyer money the buyer will be paying out whenever the charge comes due, like taxes.)
- **On rent prorations, DEBIT THE SELLER** and **CREDIT THE BUYER.** (The seller already collected a full month's rent but isn't the landlord for the entire month.)

Step Two – What is the Charge Per Day?

This depends on the type of calendar being used.

- A **statutory** or **banker's year** is a 360-day year and **every month is 30 days**.
- A **calendar year** is the normal 365-day year and normal amount of days per.

If the problem **does not specify, ALWAYS use the statutory year**.

To figure out the charge per day, simply take the total charge (whether it's annual taxes, monthly rent, etc.) and divide by either 360 or 365, depending on the calendar.

Step Three – How Many Days are Owed?

Here's where the calendar comes in. First off, **circle the close of escrow date.** For example, let's say the close of escrow date is the 15th of the month …

1	2	3	4	5	6	7
8	9	10	11	12	13	14
15	16	17	18	19	20	21
22	23	24	25	26	27	28
29	30					

Second, we need to know who "owns the close" – who owns the property and therefore is responsible for the prorated charge on the COE date. **Unless the question says otherwise, THE BUYER ALWAYS OWNS THE CLOSE.**

Finally, with that in mind, we will mark the days owed. If this was a charge paid in arrears, count up from the COE date. If it was a charge paid in advance or rents, count down from the COE.

For example, if we are talking about a rental property where the COE is the 15th and the buyer owns the closing date, the buyer is owed rent from the 15th through the end of the month, like this:

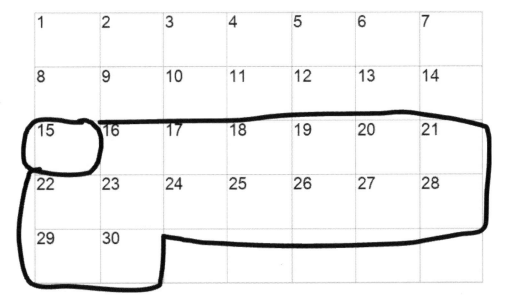

Step Four – Multiple the charge per day by the days owed

Now we put everything together. Here's our question:

> **A buyer purchases a house renting for $1,200 a month. The close of escrow is the 15th of September. Using a calendar year and the buyer owning the closing date, what is the proration?**

Step by step, here we go.

Step one – the seller is going to owe the buyer, because the buyer earns the rent from the first day they own the house.

Step two – the charge per day. Rent is $1,200 a month and there are 30 days in September:

$$1,200 \div 30 = \$40 \text{ per day}$$

Step three – count the days owed. Let's pull our calendar back down, with the close of escrow (the 15th) circled and the days the seller owes (the 15th through end of the month) marked:

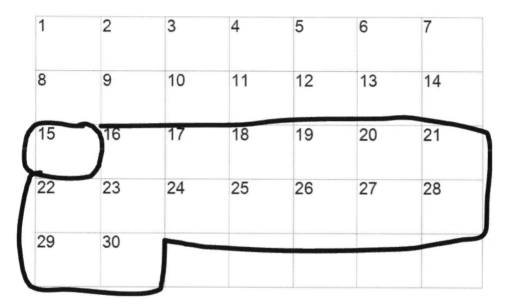

Count the days and the seller owes the buyer for 16 days.

Step four – multiply the charge per day by the number of days:

$$\$40 \times 16 \text{ days} = \$640$$

Since the seller owes, we debit the seller $640 and credit the buyer $640.

That's it!

When you practice these, take an extra minute to make sure you know who owns the closing date. Most mistakes on proration problems come from counting one day too many or too few.

The above example covers both **rent** and **HOA monthly prorations**. The only trick might be if the HOA does were paid for the year or multiple months.

That leaves …

Property Tax Prorations

Generally speaking, if the question says the seller paid something, that means that it was paid in advance. If the question doesn't say they paid, they didn't and it's a charge in arrears.

Be careful with property tax questions. First, don't assume that the taxes were paid in arrears just because that's how it's usually done. **READ THE QUESTION** to see if they were paid. Second, remember **first-half taxes** are paid on **October 1**. This payment covers taxes from January 1 to June 30. If the question says the seller **paid first half taxes** but the **close of escrow is after July 1**, <u>these still are second-half taxes being paid in arrears</u>.

On property tax problems, follow all the steps just as we described **except** you will need to add in the days for months before or after the COE, depending if the taxes were paid in arrears or advance. Arrears, count up or back to January. Advance, count down or forward to December.

Percentage Problems

The vast majority of the math of the test consists of percentage problems. You will be given two numbers and have to solve for the third. Two will be regular numbers and the third will be a percentage.

I'll explain percentage problems two different ways. Choose whichever explanation works better for you.

First, when working with percentages …

- **If you're trying to get from a larger (non-percentage) number to a smaller number, multiply by the percentage**
- **If you're trying to get from a smaller number to a larger number, divide by the percentage**

Seller's Net Proceeds

Let's use for this example a question asking about a seller's net proceeds.

> **A seller wants to net $270,000 from the sale of their home after paying a 9% commission. What do they have to sell their home for?**

First off, on math problems, **start at the end of the question**. See what you're being asked before jumping in and calculating. On this one, we need to figure out the sales price. I know you'll agree with me that the sales price is going to be more than the seller's proceeds after commission, right?

In other words, we have been given the smaller number – the net – and the percentage. Since we're going from the smaller number to the larger, looking above, we are going to divide.

The question now is what do we divide by. Here, we are going to go for a little Garanimals matching – make sure the percentage you multiply or divide by has the same label as the number you're multiplying or dividing.

The seller's going to keep $270,000. That means we need to divide that number by the percentage of the sales price the seller gets to keep. If the seller is paying a 9% commission, that means the seller is going to keep 91% of the sales price.

$$\$270,000 \div 91\% = \$296,703$$

Enter the T-Chart

The other way to solve this problem is by using a simply T-chart. You can use the T-chart on any problem with a percentage of 100 or less. The smallest number always will be on top, the largest on the left, the percentage on the right.

$$\div \frac{\text{SMALLEST}}{\text{LARGEST} \; \text{✗} \; \text{PCT}} \div$$

Enter the two numbers that you have, then either divide or multiply to get the third.

$$\div \frac{\$275,000}{\text{✗} \; 91\%} \div \qquad \div \frac{\$275,000}{\$296,703 \, \text{✗} \; 91\%} \div$$

Sellers' Net Proceeds – Variations

We've spent the past page working the basic calculation for sellers' net proceeds. The only variable here is if the question adds in closing costs.

- If closing costs are given to you as a **dollar amount**, add that to the net proceeds the seller wants **before dividing**.
- If closing costs are given to you as a **percentage of the sales price**, add that to the commission percentage **before dividing**.

If we go back to the last problem and add closing costs, it would look something like this …

> **A seller wants to net $270,000 from the sale of their home after paying a 9% commission and $15,000 in closing costs. What do they have to sell their home for?**

Since the closing costs given to us were a **dollar amount**, we are going to add that dollar amount to the net **before dividing**.

$$\$270,000 + \$15,000 = \$285,000$$
$$\$285,000 \div 91\% = \$313,186$$

Now, with the closing costs as a percentage …

> **A seller wants to net $270,000 from the sale of their home after paying a 9% commission and 3% in closing costs. What do they have to sell their home for?**

Since the closing costs given to us were a **percentage**, we are going to add that to the commission percentage **before dividing**.

$$9\% \text{ commission} + 3\% \text{ closing costs} = 12\%$$
$$100\% \text{ sales price} - 12\% = 88\% \text{ the seller gets to keep}$$
$$\$270,000 \div 88\% = \$306,818$$

Depreciation

We continue with the T-chart and percentage problems with depreciation. You can be asked about depreciation a few different ways – in terms of a loss of value, or artificially depreciating the value of a property as part of a cost approach appraisal.

Let's start with a loss of value …

> **An investor purchased a house for $200,000 three years ago and sells the house for $156,000. What was the percentage of loss?**

Start at the end to see what we are being asked – what's the percentage of loss. Now, we need to know how much money the investor lost:

$$\$200,000 - \$156,000 = \$44,000$$

Finally, to get the percentage of loss or depreciation, divide the loss by the original cost of the property. And for this, I'll go to the T-chart:

$$\div \frac{44,000}{200,000 \mid 22\%}$$

Now, I'll take the same numbers but change the problem to a cost approach appraisal:

> **An appraiser values the construction cost of a building at $200,000. Based on the condition of the property, the appraiser needs to depreciate the value 22%. What is the appraised value of the property?**

Start at the end – we need the appraised value of the property. In other words, what is the value of the property if we drop it 22% from the construction cost.

Before we go to the T-chart, make sure you know what percentage we're dividing by. **Match the labels.** If we want the appraised value – the amount leftover after depreciation – we need to divide by the percentage leftover after depreciation.

100% of construction cost – 22% depreciation = 78% remaining

Now to the T-chart:

$$\frac{\$156,000}{200,000 \; \cancel{\times} \; 78\%}$$

Appreciation

There are two flavors of appreciation problems. For the first one we are going to look at, we are given the purchase price and either the current value (percent of appreciation) or sales price (percentage of profit) and need to come up with the percentage.

A homeowner just sold their house for $320,000. They purchased the house eight years for $285,000. What was their percentage of profit?

Start at the end – we need the percentage of profit. Which means, first, we need to know what the seller's profit was:

$$\$320,000 - \$285,000 = \$35,000$$

Now we can go to the T-chart and divide the profit by the original sales price.

$$\div \frac{35,000}{285,000 \mid \textbf{12.3\%}}$$

The second typo of appreciation problem is going to be one where we can't use the T-chart. But it's still relatively easy to do as long as you remember one trick.

A homeowner just sold their house for $320,000, which includes a 12 percent profit. What was the original purchase price?

On this type of appreciation question, there's only one thing to remember: **divide the sales price by 1 + the percentage of profit.** It would look like this:

$320,000 ÷ 1.12 (one plus the percentage of profit) = $285,714

Property Tax Calculations

We went through these calculations in more detail in Chapter 7. Here is the problem that we worked there:

Q: A residential property in Phoenix has an LPV of $250,000. Phoenix has a tax rate of 4 percent. What is the property owner's tax bill?

A: $1,000. ($250,000 x 10% assessment ratio = $25,000. $25,000 x 4% tax rate = $1,000)

We also can put this on the T-chart:

$$\frac{1,000}{25,000 \; \text{✗} \; 4\%}$$

The one variable to watch for on this is if the tax rate is given in terms of 100s of assessed value. Rather than four percent, the tax rate could be presented as $4 per $100 of assessed value. Again, don't worry about figuring out how many hundreds you have, just multiply by the percentage and call it a day.

Loan Interest

Two types of questions could come up here. The first asks for the monthly interest payment on an interest-only loan. The other asks you for one payment somewhere in the middle of the loan period for an installment loan (monthly interest plus a set amount of principal.)

What is the monthly payment on a $150,000 straight loan at 5%?

Remember, straight loan is another way of saying interest-only. First, we need the annual interest. You can put it on the T-chart, but I'll write it out here:

$$\$150,000 \times 5\% = \$7,500$$

Now, the question is asking for the monthly payment, so take the annual interest and divide it by 12 to get monthly:

$$\$7,500 \div 12 = \$625$$

That's it. Not so bad, right? Now for the installment loan version:

A borrower has a $150,000 loan at 5% per annum and is paying $1,500 in principal every month. What is the fourth month's payment?

Per annum, by the way, just is a fancy way of saying annually. With an installment loan, the borrower is paying a set amount of principal every month. So, every month, the interest shrinks because there's a smaller principal balance.

If we are asked about the **fourth** month's payment, that means the borrower has paid **three** months of principal:

$$1,500 \times 3 = 4500$$

Which means our current principal balance is

$$150,000 - 4500 = 144,500$$

We know the math from here:

$$144,500 \times 5\% = 7,225$$

$$7225 \div 12 = \$602.08$$

Which makes the payment **602.08 (interest) + 1,500 (principal) for $2,102.08.**

Area and Perimeter Calculations

Remember, the **area** of a parcel is the **width times length**. Also, if the question has a reference to front footage, that is the width at the front of the lot. Area is quoted in square feet and can be converted to acreage.

An acre is 43,560 square feet. One way to remember this is **four** snowbirds driving **35** in a **60**. Welcome to life on Loop 101.

Perimeter is the length of all the sides added together. Perimeter is expressed in linear feet, and could by converted to miles (though it's unlikely.)

> **A parcel is 5,800 feet by 2,320 feet. What is the perimeter? How many acres are contained in the parcel?**

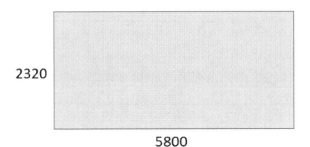

2320

5800

Area = 2320 x 5800 = 13,456,000
13,456,000 ÷ 43,560 = 308.9 acres

Perimeter = 5800 + 2320 + 5800 + 2320 = 16,240 ft

One variable that could come is a half-parcel – the parcel is in the shape of a triangle (think metes and bounds). **If the parcel is triangular, divide the area by 2.**

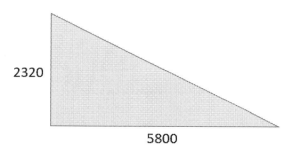

2320 x 5800 = 13,456,000
13,456,000 ÷ 2 = 6,728,000
6,728,000 ÷ 43,560 = 154.5 acres

Another variable would be an unusually shaped parcel. When presented with something like the parcel below, just reduce what you see down to rectangles and triangles and you'll be set.

Starting from the point of beginning, travel south 1,700 feet, then west 1,400 feet, the north 850 feet then back to the point of beginning.

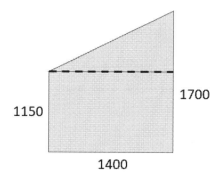

We are going to take this odd shape and turn into a rectangle and a triangle. We know that long side is 1700 feet. When we create our triangle, we're going to subtract the 1150 on the bottom for the rectangle, leaving us 550 feet up top.

That leaves us something looking like this:

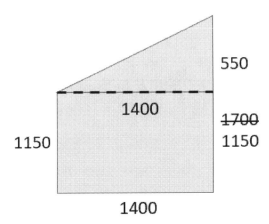

Now, calculate the square footage of each part separately:

$$1400 \times 1150 = 1,610,000$$
$$1400 \times 550 = 770,000 \div 2 = 385,000$$
$$1,610,000 + 385,000 = 1,995,000$$

And, if the question wants acreage, divide by 43,560.

Commissions

Amazingly, few students ever have trouble with commission problems, probably because that's the goal for the license. Here's a sample problem for you nevertheless:

> **What would a salesperson's commission be on a $337,000 sale if the total commission is 9% and the salesperson is on a 70/30 split with their broker?**

On a 70/30 split, the broker takes 30% and the salesperson keeps the other 70%.

$$\$337,000 \times 9\% = \$30,330$$
$$\$30,330 \times 70\% = \$21,231$$

Discount Points

Remember, discount points for our purposes are 1/8 percent reductions in the interest rate. The borrower pays 1% of the loan amount up front to lower their interest rate by 1/8 percent.

A bank will lend a borrower 90% on a $220,000 purchase at 6% interest. The borrower wants to lower their rate to 5¾%. How much would the borrower pay to do this?

First, we need the loan amount:

$$\$220,000 \times 90\% = \$198,000$$

The borrower wants to lower interest rate by ¼, which also equals 2/8 or two points. Each point will cost the borrower one percent of the loan amount.

$$\$198000 \times 2\% = \$3,960$$

Capitalization Questions

These questions deal with net operating income and capitalization rate. Putting the formula on the T-chart, it looks like this:

Plug in the two numbers you are given, the multiply or divide to get the third.

An investor paid $1,150,000 for an 8-unit apartment building and assumes a 5% vacancy rate and 3% in credit losses. Monthly rent per unit is $1,100. Annual taxes are $12,000, maintenance is $2,000 a month and the investor is depreciating the property at 4%. What is the investor's rate of return?

We'll unpack this one step by step. First, jumping to the end, what we are looking for is the investor's rate of return. We are given the value, but we need to calculate the net operating income. (A more detailed explanation is in Chapter 21.)

Start with our projected gross income:

$$\$1,100 \times 8 \text{ units} \times 12 \text{ months} = \$105,600$$

Next, we subtract our vacancies and credit losses. You can just hit the subtract key and enter the percentage on your calculator here.

$$\$105,600 - 8\% = \$96,600 \text{ effective gross income}$$

Now for operating expenses. We have taxes, maintenance and depreciation. But, if you remember what is and is not an operating expense, we never account for the depreciation because this is investor specific. It's in the question as filler.

$96,600 - $12,000 taxes - $24,000 annual maintenance = $60,600 NOI

And now, finally, the cap rate is the net operating income divided by the value of the property:

$60,600 ÷ 1,150,000 = 5.3%

Putting the calculation on the T-chart:

$$\div \frac{60,600}{1,150,000 \quad \big| \quad 5.3\%}$$

Recap
- Read the end of the question first so you know what you're being asked
- Eliminate any filler, like we did with the NOI question.
- Don't round things up or down. Use whatever number your calculator gives.
- Finally, if you can do the percentage math, do the percentage math. There are no points for style. If you need help, rely on the T-chart to get you there.

Index

About the Author

Jonathan Dalton has been a REALTOR and associate broker based in the greater Phoenix area since 2004.

Jonathan first taught continuing education classes for his brokerage in the late 2000s, and was a state-approved pre-licensing instructor for both sales associates and brokers.

Jonathan lives in the northwest Valley with his wife, Kathie, and a menagerie of dogs.

Made in the USA
Las Vegas, NV
21 June 2024